Fighting, Loving, Teaching

CONSTRUCTING KNOWLEDGE: CURRICULUM STUDIES IN ACTION
Volume No: 4

Scope

"Curriculum" is an expansive term; it encompasses vast aspects of teaching and learning. Curriculum can be defined as broadly as, "The content of schooling in all its forms" (English, p. 4), and as narrowly as a lesson plan.

Complicating matters is the fact that curricula are often organized to fit particular time frames. The incompatible and overlapping notions that curriculum involves everything that is taught and learned in a particular setting *and* that this learning occurs in a limited time frame reveal the nuanced complexities of curriculum studies.

"Constructing Knowledge" provides a forum for systematic reflection on the substance (subject matter, courses, programs of study), purposes, and practices used for bringing about learning in educational settings. Of concern are such fundamental issues as: What should be studied? Why? By whom? In what ways? And in what settings? Reflection upon such issues involves an inter-play among the major components of education: subject matter, learning, teaching, and the larger social, political, and economic contexts, as well as the immediate instructional situation. Historical and autobiographical analyses are central in understanding the contemporary realties of schooling and envisioning how to (re)shape schools to meet the intellectual and social needs of all societal members. Curriculum is a social construction that results from a set of decisions; it is written and enacted and both facets undergo constant change as contexts evolve.

This series aims to extent the professional conversation about curriculum in contemporary educational settings. Curriculum is a designed experience intended to promote learning. Because it is socially constructed, curriculum is subject to all the pressures and complications of the diverse communities that comprise schools and other social contexts in which citizens gain self-understanding.

Fighting, Loving, Teaching: An Exploration of Hope, Armed Love and Critical Urban Pedagogies

by

Emily A. Daniels, PhD

SUNY Plattsburgh, New York, USA

SENSE PUBLISHERS
ROTTERDAM/TAIPEI

A C.I.P. record for this book is available from the Library of Congress.

ISBN: 978-94-6209-072-9 (Paperback)
ISBN: 978-94-6209-073-6 (Hardback)
ISBN: 978-94-6209-074-3 (e-book)

Published by: Sense Publishers,
P.O. Box 21858,
3001 AW Rotterdam,
The Netherlands
https://www.sensepublishers.com/

Printed on acid-free paper

Firmly anchored in a critical educational tradition of struggle, Fighting, Loving, Teaching reawakens teachers to educational justice and the everyday possibilities of a pedagogy of the heart. With uncompromising passion and commitment, this timely book weaves a narrative of critical persistence and radical hope, in an effort to reinsert the revolutionary power of love into current discourses of democratic schooling and society.

Antonia Darder
Leavey Endowed Chair of Ethics and Moral Leadership
Loyola Marymount University, Los Angeles
Author of Reinventing *Paulo Freire: A Pedagogy of Love*

Emily Daniels' book contributes to the field's awareness of transformative urban teachers' practices through a rich theoretical framework and a rigorous phenomenological research methodology. In this way, her work expands our understanding of transformative teachers' experiences and practices with youth in ways that can inform practitioners, researchers, and activists alike. She draws on the work of Paulo Freire and Antonia Darder to guide her research of armed love, hope and caring in these exemplary educators' practices, providing important empirical data and analyses to a rich, largely conceptual literature with. This approach gives us a unique way to understand such educators' commitments to their students and their profession.

Dr. Nancy Ares, University of Rochester.

DEDICATION

To my ever-patient Mother and son – Nana and Santiago-Arturo.
Thank you.

TABLE OF CONTENTS

ACKNOWLEDGMENTS

This work would not have been possible without the support of my Mother; emotional, financial and practical, and the patience and love of my son, Santiago – who knows too well the long nights and "always in the middle of somethings" that Mama has been engaged in. This has been a long and tough journey, and I know that we have all made sacrifices along the way. I want to say that they have not been in vain. I also want to thank my Dad and Dana for their love and support across the miles. My best friends and kind-hearted mentors Tomás, Charlana, M., Nancy, Jeff, Ed, Antonia, Alice, and Brad.

I. INTRODUCTION

I am hopeful, not out of mere stubbornness, but out of an existential, concrete imperative. (Freire, 1992, p. 2)

Just raise your head up, and stand up, no fear in your heart, tell me love and hope never die. So raise your head up and stand up, no reason to cry 'cause your heart and soul will survive. (Ozomatli, 2004)

Urban education is a highly contested terrain which resides in our imaginations, our prejudices, and our everyday experiences. It can be utopic or dystopic; what do we see when we consider the space of urban education and the students and teachers who reside there? What are the possibilities and the "untested feasibilities" (Freire, 2005)?

The purpose of this book is to explore urban teachers' praxis with historically marginalized youth, in response to the multifaceted challenges facing urban youth, educators, and communities. As a scholar with a strong interest in Paulo Freire's (1970, 1992, 2005, 2007) work and that of other critical pedagogical scholars, my research adds to the empirical literature on critical pedagogy, while bringing in the lens of caring and hope to deepen the discussion. Additionally, exploring and defining the concept of "armed love" was central to my work with these exemplary urban educators. Darder (2003) defines this as, "a love that could be lively, forceful, and inspiring, while at the same time, critical, challenging and insistent" (p. 497).

My work also examined what is "going right" with teachers and marginalized youth rather than what is "going wrong". Ginwright (2006) points to the pathological focus of social science research done on Black youth in particular as being problematic. He argues that by virtue of its sole concentration on the *problems* within poor Black communities, the research itself reiterates negativity and is limited by being overly deterministic in its focus, and disallowing for the positive and transformative aspects of Black youth culture.

Another example of this discourse of deficiency at a larger level, would be the "achievement gap" discussions which assign an inherent level of superiority to white students and a subordinate position to students of color in test-taking (and by inference intelligence) measurements. When African American, Latino and Native American students don't "measure up", Eurocentric measuring tools and assumptions have not generally been questioned, but rather Black and Brown youth become the focus of deficit discourses. There are many scholars who challenge these notions (see Ladson-Billings, 2006 and Cross, 2007 for provocative and insightful discussions of the "achievement gap") and their work is a powerful reminder of the insidious damage possible through descriptions that privilege whiteness while denying Black and Brown youth the opportunities to be viewed and treated as successful, intelligent and gifted. Though these discussions can seem shocking, from a Critical Race Theoretical (CRT) standpoint, racism is portrayed as endemic to American society, and is seen as closely intertwined with all aspects of American-ness, in our cultural beliefs, practices, and within our institutions (Ladson-Billings, 2003, Dixson & Rousseau, 2006, Delgado& Stefancic, 2000; Solórzano, Ceja & Yosso, 2000). The statistics for youth of color continue to be disturbing; when we "lose" our precious children to the streets, the prisons, and the military complex, we can see waves of complex, multilayered injustices that seem overwhelming.

Setting

Rosa Parks (Parks) high school is located in a North-eastern post-industrial city that hosts numerous coffee shops, an incredible art gallery, restaurants, and a plethora of summer festivals. Our city has a variety of challenges as well as incredible opportunities within it. These opportunities are not equally available to everyone, and there are remarkably sharp divisions based on race, class and zip code. For instance, the city school district (CSD) has high numbers of students receiving of free and reduced lunch. According to their website, 84% of students are eligible to take part in the free and reduced lunch program. The rate of high school graduation is also distressing, ranging between 37% and 55% for 2009, which is described as "increasing, but still too low." These challenges are also augmented by the deindustrialization of the city, with its major economic corporations having downsized and/or relocated.

Within this setting, schools operate and attempt to negotiate the multiple difficulties that can arise. Rosa Parks high-school is located downtown, near a section of the city with a bar, a food cooperative, a donut shop or two, and a complicated highway intersection that cuts through and around what I assume used to be neighborhoods. There are approximately 180 students who attend this school, which serves grades 9 -12. The students are predominantly African American, and there are Latino and White students represented as well. It is a special school, in its approach to learning as being "more than just a test score", and it is also a member of the Coalition of Essential Schools (CES). This entails a distinctive approach to education focusing on individual students, the development and nurturance of learners, and a democratic approach to education.

The Problem

Education, and schools in particular, are sites of struggle (Nieto, 2005; Nieto, 2003; Apple, 1990; Kohn, 1999; Tyack & Cuban, 1995; Freire, 1970/1993; Duncan-Andrade & Morrell, 2008; Kincheloe, 2007). These struggles and battles are multifaceted: loaded with politics, ideologies and warring factions. Opposing arguments are presented and debated, such as: schools need improvement, education is hopeless, education is for freedom, education is for oppression, more government involvement, less government involvement, smaller schools, better methods, more testing, less testing. The list of demands and solutions is strongly contested and deeply polarizing, but within our society many believe that something is wrong with schools, teachers, and/or students. When the government becomes involved through *No Child Left Behind* (NCLB) and other "well-intended" legislated attempts to "fix" schools, these instances have often had undesired and even disastrous effects that have increased inequities instead of counteracting them (Kohn, 1999; Hursh, 2007; Harris, 2007). Despite fervent critiques and questionable "reforms" and "solutions," problems persist and inequities continue. This is notable in our "standards" driven era of simplified conceptualizations of learning as easily measurable and connected to corporate-created tests.

This is especially true in urban schools for youth of color; schooling is not only contested, but inherently unequal (Kozol, 2005; Ginwright, Cammarota & Noguera, 2005; Duncan-Andrade & Morrell, 2008). Schools are often sites of domination, control and oppression for youth of color, not spaces of learning or equity (Ladson-Billings, 1994; Cammarota, 2007; Delgado Bernal, 2002). Within the last 25 years these circumstances have been exacerbated: the emphasis on standardized testing and scores, inequitable district funding formulas, and classed and racialized re-segregation within districts have contributed to a despairing and demoralizing perspective on schooling as well as a host of negative implications for teachers and students (Kozol, 1991; Janesick, 2006; Darder, 2002; Lipman, 2002; Nieto, 2003).

In addition to these complexities, the problems of representation and power have plagued debates about justice and equity within schools. Frequently these discussions have been rooted in deficit models that not only deny white privilege and structural racism, but lay the blame for injustice and inequities on the hearts, minds, and souls of those who have been victimized and demonized by it (Akom, 2008; Lipsitz, 2005; Weiner, 2007). As stated by Lorde (2007), "The oppressors maintain their position and evade responsibility for their own actions" (p. 53). These discourses arose partly from historical factors that laid the foundation of racism in the construction of our Constitution and the blood of the oppressed that has gone into the creation of our country. Much more recently, we find the "culture of poverty" model developed and perpetuated by scholars anxious to problematize and blame Brown and Black folk in an unjust and pathologizing manner (Akom, 2008). This has a long and tragic interconnection to our shared history in the United States. For centuries, we have suffered the consequences of the creation of a country so clearly based in racialized discourses that denied the humanity of the Indigenous, Latino/a and African American people, we have suffered the ramifications of this for centuries (Ladson-Billings, 2003). The genocidal treatment of the Native Americans, the dispossession and assault against Latino/as, and the residue of slavery have all left their marks on our society, effects which endure into the present.

These historical effects linger in the continued practices of institutional, societal and individual racism that are ingrained within our culture, and are normalized in their continued persistence. The discourses that arose during the 1950s and 1960s within the U.S. were an extension of this, with the deficit model applied to all who were not middle class and white. Many scholars argue that these racist undercurrents still exist, but, like a virus, have mutated into different forms of display and enactment in the post 1960's United States (Bonilla-Silva & Embrick, 2006). These discourses are much more difficult to trace in contrast to the older paradigms that previously defined what racism entails. One of the main points is that racism is still normalized and experienced by people of color within our society, but is much more masked in its display by terms and concepts such as "color-blindness" and "reverse racism" (Bonilla-Silva & Embrick, 2006; Solórzano, Ceja & Yosso, 2000).

I argue in the Freirean tradition that we as teachers need to be both critically engaged and (radically) loving simultaneously; that these are linked to transformative education, and that hope is closely connected to creating different possibilities for education in an inequitable world. In a piece that was published posthumously by Freire's wife (2007), there is a beautiful point that Freire makes about the importance of dreaming: "My discourse in favor of dreaming, of utopia, of freedom, of democracy is the discourse of those who refuse to settle and do not allow the taste for being human, which fatalism deteriorates, to die within themselves" (p. 26). In order to avoid the destructive and oppressive tendencies of education, we desperately need spaces for liberatory praxis. Education is inherently political (Apple, 1990; Freire, 2005; hooks, 1994) and the choices we make as educators to move toward socially aware and activist stances have an important place in our classrooms and curricula, and for the children with whom we work.

Research Exploration

I believe that teachers and their classrooms can conceive and demonstrate pedagogical praxis that involves both reflection and transformative action that is based on and intertwined with a deep political love for children, and this love is connected to the hope necessary to persevere despite barriers. Freire (2004) and Darder (2002) define hope as central to the transformative experience of education. Freire takes this even further to argue that, "hope is an ontological need" (p. 2). I argue that, especially in a field such as education, with the daily interactions and challenges of balancing public opinion, institutional racism, and shortages of funding and respect, hope is a necessity for both teachers and the youth with whom they work. I also believe that, in part, the militant/radical love of teachers intertwined with hope, offers a spiritual and practical antidote to these challenges, and that classrooms can be both protective and nurturing spaces for youth. The problems are many: perceptions and realities of schools in a racist and divided society, high push/drop-out rates, unfair tracking practices, and unsafe schools. Amid these issues lie the precarious positions of our children, especially those in low income areas (Duncan-Andrade & Morrell, 2008).

In response to these complexities, my goal within this work was to explore the role of hope, armed love and "praxis" in the work of transformative teachers of marginalized children and youth. More specifically, I examined the conception and implementation of caring, armed love, hope, and critical pedagogy.

Significance of Research

Critical social theories are excellent at providing critiques; however they must not simply stop at the theoretical and philosophical presentation of the negativity that abounds in education and in the daily lives of urban youth. This can lead to despair, and it is a delicate and tenuous balance between admitting the challenges and at the same time presenting alternatives that are empowering, without surrendering or sounding unrealistically idealistic. In fact, many academics that I have encountered perceive hope or optimism as symptoms of a misplaced naïveté, instead of powerful sources of change-agency. Urban education is a complicated space, and has many different facets within it that are connected to historical inequalities and current social injustices. In terms of the challenges faced by young people of color, Ginwright, Cammarota and Noguera (2005) state:

> Global capitalism has contributed to the exodus of jobs, higher levels of inequality, and the marginalization of the urban poor. Urban youth have been particularly affected by this transformation and the concomitant social and economic conditions. (p. 24)

The speeches of politicians are a superficial start, especially in the face of many complexities. We must bring this rhetoric into concrete practice for children of all colors and classes, youth *are* our future. Ngũgĩ (1993) eloquently and chillingly states:

> Children are the future of any society. If you want to know the future of a society look at the eyes of the children. If you want to maim the future of any society, you simply maim the children. Thus the struggle for the survival of our children is the struggle for the survival of our future. (p. 76)

Although we *must* face the demons of inequity that continue to torment our children, we can *choose* our response to them. As educators we have the responsibility to be aware of the politics we are choosing, and to what end they are directed. Are our positions coming from the politics of despair and nihilism, or are they the politics of movement and hope? Where does change originate and what sustains it? Do we believe that education and educators can make a difference in the lives of children and youth, or not? Even amid postmodern debates that de-center the individual as connected only to larger systems, we need to consider the everyday realities of youth and children we work with.

Explorations of caring, armed love, and critical pedagogies.

I hope to present the many ways in which the difficulties and challenges reside alongside the promising possibilities for resistance. In the midst of chaos and inequity, there must be room for growth and movement, for a re-visioning of what could be possible.

Chapter 2 goes into depth regarding the extensive literature on caring, armed love and critical pedagogies. Through the second chapter, I aim to present the many different instances and representations of caring and armed love, as well as problematize them, and the implementation of these standpoints. Caring and love seem like "simple" concepts, but the literature reveals a wide range of understandings and perspectives on these concepts. Hope and critical pedagogies are also examined.

Chapter 3 discusses the theoretical framework (a combination of caring, armed love, and critical pedagogy) and the methodology used to implement the research. (Armed love is based in the tradition of Paulo Freire (2005) and Antonia Darder (2002, 2003). Through defining and examining armed love, I argue that it includes a strongly critical and activist stance that is intertwined with the core commitment to changing the lives of students through transformative education. The methodology I chose involved a qualitative case study with interview and video components, based in the work of Stake (1995) and Seidman (2006).

Chapters 4 and 5 focus on the multitude of findings including the importance of understanding, relationship, community and caring, the salience of race, hope and despair, as well as armed love. The findings present some fascinating and powerful contrasts from these educators' experiences which help us to understand the complexities of urban education and critical pedagogies, as well as armed love and caring.

Chapter 6 concludes the work by drawing parallels to larger social forces of oppression and the ways that individuals must continue to struggle despite the need for larger and deeper changes to occur. There is resistance, criticality, hope, despair, opportunity and stories of struggle to be common unifying themes within the practices of these exemplary educators.

First, I will begin with questions, background, and problems to proceed into the realm of urban education more deeply. Education is immersed in ideologies, politics, racism, power, privilege and dominance. In the midst of these social forces, children and teachers struggle to survive and to thrive. They negotiate and create caring spaces in the face of tremendous difficulties.

WHAT'S LOVE GOT TO DO WITH CARING, HOPE AND CRITICAL PEDAGOGIES?

It is impossible to teach without the courage to love, without the courage to try a thousand times before giving up. In short, it is impossible to teach without a forged, invented and well-thought-out capacity to love. (Freire, 2005, p. 5)

"Love" is a common word, but its definitions, experiences and representations differ greatly. This terminology and its classroom application vary greatly depending on the researcher, teacher and students- as well as culturally specific connotations. Definitions of terms such as *love, hope, caring* and *critical pedagogy* are potentially sites of contestation. These terms and their demonstration can be sites of growth or of conflict, and exploring them brings greater understanding of the complexities involved.

Forms of Love

According to hooks (2003), "at its best teaching is a caring profession" (p. 86). If caring is so intimately interwoven into teaching, it is necessary to discover what is meant by caring, and this proves to be a challenging task. Caring has different aspects, and the definition is a challenge because of the orientation, experiences and many perspectives on caring.

Noddings' (1984, 2002) work on caring is seminal. She wrote from a white second-wave Feminist standpoint on the importance of caring as intertwined with morality and ethics. Her work examined and expanded on different aspects of caring, bringing a much needed discussion of caring into the field. Noddings connects caring to fundamental needs and human connections, and makes a strong argument that both defines what genuine caring looks like and points to its necessity in our interactions. Her conception of caring also noted the importance of the care-giver and the cared for as equally crucial elements of caring relationships.

Noddings' work presents a nuanced perspective of caring, but subscribes to a common mistake associated with the time period; it universalized women's experience as white and middle class, and 'naturally' connected to caring. This assumption that caring is based in biology or gender is limited in its notion of what caring is, and polarizes the sexes based on this perceived strength (or weakness) in demonstrating caring. Her work is still quite useful when considered with an understanding of its limitations. It contributes a particular foundation to the discussion of caring which is elaborated by many other scholars in a wide range of fields, including education.

Other scholars have expanded on Noddings' work (see Goldstein & Lake, 2000, 2003; Haskell McBee, 2007; Cassidy & Bates, 2005; Thompson, 1998; Valenzuela, 1999; Lysaker, McCormick & Brunette, 2004; Beauboeuf-

Lafontant, 2002, 2005; Antrop-González & De Jesús, 2006; Ladson-Billings, 1994; Rolón Dow, 2005). Haskell McBee (2007) found seven themes in particular surfaced through her research that can assist with a definition of what caring means to teachers specifically: offering help, showing compassion, showing interest, caring about the individual, giving time, listening and getting to know students (p. 36). Other work, such as that by Shel (2006) equates caring learning environments with nurturing students' growth and ties it to both cognitive and emotional development. Cassidy and Bates (2005) described caring as both a "perspective and practice" (p. 68). Citing Noddings' (1984) work extensively, they see caring as having holistic effects on youth and children when it is implemented with a focus on containing different components. According to these authors, the special challenges of the school (which worked with youth who had been identified as having difficult life situations) are contradicted by the, "ambience of the school, which exuded peacefulness and warmth. Students who had been labelled unmanageable, even violent, by former schools and by the justice system appeared happy and relaxed and were doing schoolwork" (p. 72). As demonstrated by these works, caring can manifest and impact classrooms very differently. Caring relationships can be critical to the learner in their growth, as well as their success in school, it can even possibly negate challenging environments and situations for youth.

Caring concepts which build deeply on the work of Noddings (such as those above) can be problematic, however. Though these pieces offer a direction to begin to investigate the definitions of caring, they are notably quiet on the ethnic/racial/class implications or assumptions behind the conceptions of caring. There is a need to examine other studies that challenge the concepts and assumptions of caring that are grounded in experiences of white privilege. In fact, Thompson's (1998) work explicitly challenges the ethic of caring (and Noddings' previous work) as Eurocentric and subscribing to an ideology of color-blindness. This is important to understand because caring can vary so greatly, and so much of the caring literature is based on Noddings' work.

Thompson traces the origins of the theories of caring to Carol Gilligan's (1977) work *In a Different Voice*. Thompson's critique begins by pointing to the fact that, "Black feminist theorists and other scholars have long argued that the values that appear natural and universal to Whites are values that *work* for Whites, including White feminists" (p. 526). Thompson posits that by virtue of the lack of questioning of the concepts of care, approaching this as a universal is dangerous. Through doing so, difference becomes minimized and absorbed into the (white) discourse. Caring becomes essentially "whitewashed", disregarding the nuances and differences in communities of color.

The whiteness of the caring literature is challenged by other scholars as well. Valenzuela (1999) realized the interconnection between youth's perceptions of teachers as caring or uncaring and their connections to school and desire to achieve. She was careful to present the conflicting definitions of caring as understood by students and teachers, mentioning specifically that *educación* is a foundational concept connected to caring for Mexican and Mexican-American youth, and that the definition of *educación* is important to them. She states:

Educación is a conceptually broader term than its English language cognate. It refers to the family's role of inculcating in children a sense of moral, social, and personal responsibility and serves as the foundation for all other learning. Though inclusive of formal academic training, *educación* additionally refers to competence in the social world, wherein one respects the dignity and individuality of others. (p. 23)

Caring is interconnected to culture, to morality and to *genuine* relationships and understanding of students. Valenzuela (1999) argues that authentic relationships of caring with students are central to success. By not establishing these genuine connections, the mostly Anglo teachers were denying the importance of students' cultural backgrounds and also created a "subtractive" schooling environment for the youth in her work. The schooling environment acted as a destructive force for the youth enmeshed within it, due to the lack of caring and culturally-based relationships.

Visions and praxis of caring and armed love.

The works below move towards armed love in their approaches to student-teacher relationships. It is sometimes difficult to separate the differences between what caring and armed love manifest as, especially since the literature has very few studies that touch on armed love explicitly. However, the research mentioned in this section uses other terms that coincide with the goals of armed love. The political elements in the search for equity and the highly-demanding nature of armed love are shown here.

Antrop-González and De Jesús (2006) present their research and description of caring with a focus on socioculturally situated caring in two Latino community schools. In this case caring was contextually situated within the respective Latino communities, and connected with social activism and empowerment as well as struggles for equity. The authors based their work substantially on both Thompson (1998) and Valenzuela (1999). Their conceptions of caring are connected to justice. Their discussion included powerful examples of personally and politically relevant curricula for Latino youth who attend the schools. In particular, one concept based in Latino culture, *personalismo,* was connected to the schools' institutional practice. The authors cite Santiago-Rivera et al. (as cited in Antrop-González and De Jesús, 2006) and describe this as an emphasis on personal connections, warmth, and close relationships.

Brown (2009) examined African American men's teaching styles as performance, and found some powerful themes. Brown approaches pedagogy as "performative", and looks at the nuanced versions of interaction that African American teachers in his study demonstrate. In his findings, he points to three distinct patterns of performance; "Enforcement", "Playfulness" and "Negotiation" as key elements. Each of these styles was flexible and changed depending on situations. This connects to armed love, in the interactional basis of connections between teachers and students, as well as a form of directness in communication.

Ware (2006) defines advocacy, political awareness and caring as *Warm Demander Pedagogy* (p. 427). Care-giving is one of the notable roles that African American teachers take on. Within her framework of *Warm Demanders* as defined by Vasquez (as cited in Ware, 2006) teachers who work well with students of color are seen as simultaneously having affection and high expectations and demands for the youth they work with. Ware categorized her participants within three different contexts: authority figures, care givers and pedagogues (p. 436), and provided examples from her research to support these observations. Caring and strong discipline were intertwined here with high expectations for youth, similar to the ways in which I have envisioned and examined armed love.

Roberts (2010) develops her theory of *culturally relevant critical teacher care*, which she connects with the teaching practices of African American teachers. She looks at the perceptions as well as the embodiment of caring in relation to African American students. Her predominant themes spoke of "political clarity/colour[sic] talk and concern for students' futures" (p. 455). These themes engaged open, honest discussion and guidance in dealing with racism, as well as encouraging students to consider possible careers, and to navigate away from the dangers which they may face in their lives. Race, advocacy and caring are intertwined here.

Foster (1992) discussed the pedagogical and professional experiences of African American teachers, and states, "despite the difficult circumstances in which teachers often find themselves, it is possible to consciously embrace an educational philosophy and fashion a pedagogy designed to counteract oppression and foster empowerment" (p. 179).

The analysis and presentation of caring and armed love here are based in non-Eurocentrically based frameworks, and emphasize the strengths of seeing the ethic of caring as highly flexible and powerful. Caring is contested and contextual. In this case, the form of nurturing and care are connected to both the individual students and the larger historical and social meanings to which students of color are connected. Caring and armed love involve vastly different perceptions and enactment depending on the sociocultural location of the teacher, researcher and students.

As mentioned previously, caring is complicated. Based on the works that I have encountered, as well as my own experience with transformative teachers, I have crafted the definition of armed love to build on the previous literature and to include a strong and deep commitment to protecting, caring for, and empowering students in the face of social barriers and oppressions that surface in their everyday lives, as well as a political passion to inspire and support marginalized youth. By this definition, armed love includes a strongly critical, political and activist stance that involves a deep social awareness of injustice, and the core commitment to changing the lives of historically marginalized students through transformative education. This love "looks larger" and "sees deeper" into the bigger implications beyond the classroom as well as within it. As stated by Freire: "It is indeed necessary, however, that this love be an 'armed love' the fighting love of those convinced of the right and the duty to fight, to denounce, and to announce" (p. 74). Radical, transformative approaches to education are inherently connected to the struggle for social justice, and love is a key element within this. Freire's work stressed the importance of love to teaching (2005). In fact, Freire (2005) saw love as a crucial ingredient for teachers, associating love with courage and considering it an absolute necessity.

Hope

> On the other hand- while I certainly cannot ignore hopelessness as a concrete entity, nor turn a blind eye to the historical, economic and social reasons that explain hopelessness- I do not understand human existence, and the struggle needed to improve it, apart from hope and dream... Hopelessness is but hope that has lost its bearings... (Freire, 1992, p. 2)

Freire (2004) and Darder (2002) define hope as central to the transformative experience of education. Freire takes this even further to argue that "hope is an ontological need" (p. 2) because without it, our activism dies, as we can imagine nothing better than what we see before us. Nieto (2003) posits that hope comes from a variety of sources for teachers, including from their students, colleagues, their own beliefs and refinement of their work and also from the deep belief in the optimistic possibilities of public education (with a healthy cynicism and awareness of inequities). She states that this is a difficult balance to achieve- holding onto hope despite the crushing disappointments that plague public education.

Hope and teaching are addressed in various ways in educational research including "audacious hope in action" (Givens Generett & Hicks, 2004; Givens-Generett, 2005), hope and organizational connections connected to teachers' loyalty and commitment (Hodge & Ozag, 2007), hopeful curriculum as a framework for social change and educational interventions (Renner & Brown, 2006; Renner, 2009), as well as an examination of the concept of "robust hope" in theory and practice (McInerney, 2007), and a discussion of different forms of hope in connection to urban education (Duncan-Andrade, 2009). However, despite this variety of discussions of hope, none of these works examined hope in combination with armed love and praxis. Neither have there been many empirical studies, so hope tends to be discussed much more conceptually and philosophically, and examined much less empirically.

Some authors address hope auto-ethnographically. hooks (1994) speaks of her own experience in Black schools as a child in the segregated South, with education being a hopeful endeavor in a lengthy struggle. The Black women teachers provided the challenge and support for children that they connected with in their classrooms. hooks states that:

> For Black folks teaching-education- was fundamentally political because it was ~~ruling or~~ rooted in antiracist struggle... we learned early on that our devotion to learning, ~~dominant in a~~ to a life of the mind was a counter-hegemonic act, a fundamental way to resist ~~political or~~ every strategy of white racial colonization. (p. 2) ~~societal context~~

Vitally important for this type of revolutionary educational activism is the combination of social awareness of racism and other inequities with willingness to take action for change. This is similar to Freire's concept of "praxis" (Freire, 1970/1993) which brings together critical consciousness and self-reflection with active practice. To enact transformation I argue that hope is a necessary ingredient and that its opposite, despair, leaves no room for activism or movement because of the sense of the overwhelming power of the obstacles in our way as educators. Hope creates room for movement, for possibilities to create different outcomes, whereas despair simply shuts them down. I strongly agree that hope in fact creates spaces of possibility that can open teachers and their students to new ways of being educators and educated. This hopeful vision of the present and future is vital.

Hope offers us possibilities, as mentioned by Coté, Day and de Peuter (2007), "the crucial task of our times is not only to analyze and oppose existing forms of oppression and inequality, but to discover within our various communities the powers that will allow us to create viable alternatives to them." (p. 332). To struggle, we need to be able to envision something better and more promising in our future. Hope is one element, while critical pedagogy is another potentially rich method of doing so. In the following section I will investigate the possibilities of this perspective and its valuable classroom implications.

Critical Pedagogy

Critical pedagogy is a complex approach that involves liberation through education. It has been seen as an outgrowth of Freire's (1970, 1992, 2005) work (with many other influential thinkers throughout the 20th Century) and seeks to implement particular democratic and critical educational approaches and perspectives within classroom settings (McLaren, 1999; Bartlett, 2005). McLaren (2009) states that "Critical pedagogy is fundamentally concerned with understanding the relationship between power and knowledge" (p. 72).

Historically, Freire is strongly connected with critical pedagogical approaches, however critical pedagogy also owes a debt to the larger field of critical educational thought with the Frankfurt School, which developed in Germany in the early 1920s (Darder, Baltodano & Torres, 2003). The Frankfurt School's basis in Marxism was originally focused on critiques of the historical and political environment at the beginning of the twentieth century with advanced Capitalism, domestic and international wars, and intense political struggles forming the backdrop for their philosophical and theoretical standpoints (Darder, Baltodano & Torres, 2003). The implementation of education as social critique, as well as the potential for political and social activism are the underlying currents within critical pedagogy. It is also inherently contextually based. Kincheloe (2007) argues that critical pedagogical approaches must be cognizant of the complexities of context, that "no simple, universally applicable answers can be provided to the questions of justice, power and praxis that haunt us" (p. 16).

Within our current society, where standardization and capital take precedence, critical pedagogy offers a site of potential hope and change. Critical pedagogical approaches value education as a site of social change while incorporating the criticisms of gross inequalities that continue to plague our society, its institutions, and the people attempting to survive within it.

The literature for critical pedagogical approaches varies widely with a range of practitioners and theoretical standpoints. Transformation and critique are underlying threads within this standpoint. While the critiques are crucial, I argue that hope and armed love and commitment are also necessary components. These components push the critiques further into action when practitioners run into despairing social and educational realities. All the same, critical pedagogy is powerful and interconnected to classroom practice. As argued by Lynn and Jennings (2009), critical pedagogical work is based on several important tenets, and those educators engaged in it:

(1) Question the links between knowledge and power. (2) Recognize the dialectical nature of oppression as a dehumanizing force that requires some level of 'participation' from their students. (3) Believe that dialogue and reflection are key ways to empower students in the classroom. (4) View their students are 'producers' of knowledge with the ability to transform oppressive social and cultural structures. (p. 176)

When educators are aware of the political nature of education, and practice with the knowledge and skills to use critical pedagogical approaches, they are using the classroom as a site of struggle and resistance. The classroom can become an "enclave" in otherwise uncomfortable, boring and oppressive schooling situations, especially for youth of color.

Pedagogical approaches and the choices that teachers make about them can make a difference in the lives of their/our students. Educators have power within their classrooms and institutions to make choices about what and how they teach, despite demoralizing and punitive curricular pressures. These choices that teachers make can move students toward acceptance of the status quo or toward awareness, resistance and activism in fighting against it through critique and transformation.

Classroom-based critical pedagogical interventions.

Within the past few years there has been a tremendous amount of research on practices involving critical pedagogy in the classroom (see Cammarota & Romero, 2011; Low, 2011; Lopez, 2011; Duncan-Andrade & Morrell, 2008; Lynn & Jennings, 2009; Chapman & Hobbel, 2010; McGee, 2011; Sensoy, 2011; Choudhury & Share, 2012). Authors have worked within classrooms and other spaces to engage the tenets of critical pedagogy actively with youth and adults. Though critical pedagogy has seen criticism regarding it being "overly theoretical", it is now moving firmly into the discussion and practice. The studies below examine many possibilities within the classroom for critical pedagogy and its concrete implementation.

McGee (2011) examines and reflects on the incorporation of critical pedagogy as a student teacher, addressing concepts and issues of immigration in her sixth grade classroom. She facilitates a student-generated topic, and helps her students discuss, reflect on, and learn more about issues of immigration in their school and larger society. She reflects on the ways critical pedagogy needs to be fostered in our practices, and the potential power it can bring to the classroom and students' understandings. Critical approaches can open up the minds and worlds of our youth.

Duncan-Andrade and Morrell (2008) argue that through combining criticality and practice, we find more empowering ways to bring critical pedagogy into education. The main focus of their book, *The art of critical pedagogy: Possibilities for moving from theory to practice in urban schools* is to examine and discuss the practical aspects of utilizing critical pedagogy. One example given in the incorporation of critical pedagogy is the way the teacher/researchers engage canonical literature, in combination with critical approaches. They utilized works such as *Beowulf* and *The Adventures of Huckleberry Finn* as pathways into the dominant cultural representations, while also giving the youth involved the tools to empower themselves as critical readers and be able to challenge the silent authority of these texts.

Low (2011) focuses on hip-hop and the intricacies which arise when centering hip-hop as a pedagogical approach. She examines three urban classrooms, where hip-hop was utilized as a means of examining the many layers and meanings of a critical hip-hop pedagogy. Her reflection and analysis center the ways in which race, identity, youth culture, power and expression can offer sites of conflict as well as growth for youth and those who work with them. She courageously engages with the controversies and multiple meanings of language and power through hip hop as a site of resistance and learning. As she begins her work, the core of hip-hop authenticity is explored, and then she proceeds to examine a talent night rap, where the many complex themes and interpretations of language, poetry and youth perspectives collided. This study also examines the problematic issues with language and representation within hip-hop and points to the ways in which critical hip-hop pedagogies are embraced and challenged within the curriculum. She argues that incorporating critical hip-hop pedagogies involves struggle and serious commitment by educators, parents and administrators.

The collected essays in Chapman and Hobbel (2010) examine social justice educational approaches across various disciplines, theoretically and historically. In this case, the terminology is not identical, but the practices are embodiments of critical pedagogical approaches, referring to "social justice education". The book speaks to the historical moments which have led to social justice pedagogies, including the aftermath of WWII and the Universal Declaration of Human Rights, the Civil Rights movements, Multicultural Education, the work of Freire, laboratory schools, and other social movements. They incorporate theoretical bases for critical education, and then focus on possibilities for classrooms across multiple disciplines. The final section of the book genuinely integrates social justice pedagogy through discussions and examples of instances where it has been used within classrooms from art, to ESL, to math, to science. The conclusion argues for the desperate importance of critical social education, as the need for this in a fragmented and inequitable society is pressing.

Hill (2009) also utilized youth culture and literacy practices through hip hop. The specific course he examined and also co-taught was entitled *Hip-Hop Lit,* and was an English elective. The space that he created in his classroom made a place for students to not only connect their lived experiences with the lyrics and meaning of hip-hop, but to share their own personal (and sometimes very painful) narratives as well as build a community. The lessons from this piece involved the importance of critical pedagogy with an awareness of the difficulties that we may be presenting to our students when we work with justice-centered issues, as they can bring both transformative influences as well as suffering. This is a delicate and necessary balance.

Kumashiro (2000) addresses this specifically when discussing his own teaching against oppression, when students began to struggle with and confront the power of oppression less on an intellectual level, and more on an emotional one. As he describes his students' engagement with the emotional and psychological aspects of oppression, he could see that students were put into crisis. Through this crisis, Kumashiro argues, students and teacher are in a process of "unlearning". Only by engaging with our emotions and whole selves can we expect to be fully present to help learners move through the difficult waters of oppression and critical pedagogy, of which suffering is inherently an aspect.

Sensoy (2011) speaks of an exploration of representations by seventh-graders of racism, classism and sexism. In this instance, the students were given a disposable camera and several days with explicit instructions to document instances of these particular oppressions. The student responses ranged in complexity reflecting troubling notions of the persistent divide between "school knowledge" and "life knowledge".

Darder (2002) and Nieto (2003) specifically explore the voices of teachers in their own praxis as critical educators, with excerpts from their own lives and experiences as the basis for discussion within their respective works. The voices of the teachers give a picture of their own realities, beliefs and motivations in enacting critical pedagogy, bringing critical pedagogy concretely into practice. For many of them, their lived experiences have informed their teaching and internal drive for social justice for the children (or adults) they work with, and their own praxis is the mirror of this.

Schultz (2007) worked with urban 5th graders to brainstorm, identify, and then tackle serious deficiencies in their school atmosphere and facilities. Though the author does not concretely identify his pedagogy as critical, the elements of critical pedagogy are certainly evident: relevance to the lives of the (historically marginalized) students, a critique of systemic and everyday inequities, and an activist approach to empower youth to challenge these problems. The youth developed skills in campaigning, publicity, advocacy and research as well as academic skills that are intertwined with this. Through their dedicated and thorough labor, the young participants also secure some definitive changes such as badly needed repairs for their school building.

Cammarota (2007) offers another perspective on approaches to critical pedagogy and teaching through socially relevant curriculum. His focus is specifically on Latina/o students and he argues for critical consciousness to be developed through "active participation of Latina/o students in their lives, communities and futures" (p. 87). Cammarota argues that the findings of this study showed that students who were involved felt that they were thinking differently about their own education and potential, as well as being helped to graduate from high school and consider the possibility of attending college.

External to classroom based critical pedagogical interventions.

Classrooms are only one possible venue for this kind of critical exploration. Outside of the classroom many youth-based community groups also organize, educate and unite around the themes prevalent in critical pedagogy. Some examples of these include Kwon (2008), Blackburn (2005), Chávez and Soep (2005), Ginwright (2006), Kirshner (2008), and Akom, Cammarota and Ginwright (2008), Fox, (2011/2012) and Ginwright, (2009). These works look at community groups, or critical media projects that are often youth-led as well as youth-focused, and practice critical pedagogical approaches to sharing knowledge and skills with youth to encourage local change.

One interesting example by Guajardo, Guajardo and Casaperalta (2008) focused on a hybrid site, an educational non-profit center based in a Texas high school. This organization began with an explicit focus on college preparation of Mexican American youth, and blossomed into a more holistic educational approach. The authors describe their work through focusing on the lived experiences of a young girl-participant and chronicle the development of the center through her journey through the program. Here we can see the centrality of caring and connection with critical pedagogical approaches. For example, Carmen, the focus of this work, mentioned a memory of ninth grade where students were debating a piece published in a journal that they created with their teachers. This journal work was focused on their own stories and histories, an excellent example of drawing on students' experiences to support them and to create new knowledge.

Marri and Walker (2007) examined a program that took place in a series of workshops to discuss the continuing legacy of the *Brown versus Board* decision on its 50th anniversary. In this case, New York City high-school students were the participants in an educational endeavor designed with the critical pedagogical goals of examining social movements in the past and the present.

Another aspect of critical approaches is critical literacy. This perspective views the world through a lens which includes awareness of power imbalances and the complexities and situated nature of texts, as well as the reading and writing of them. Mulcahy (2008) eloquently argues:

> Critical literacy is a mindset; it is a way of viewing and interacting with the world, not a set of teaching skills and strategies. From a pedagogical perspective, critical literacy is a philosophy that recognizes the connections between power, knowledge, language and ideology, and recognizes the inequalities and injustices surrounding us in order to move toward transformative action and social justice. (p. 16)

Moving toward creating possibilities takes courage, persistence and the realization that this struggle goes beyond us, both stretching into the past and into the future. Greene (2003) poses some eloquent and crucial questions, "How can we awaken others to possibility and the need for action in the name of possibility? How can we communicate the importance of opening spaces in the imagination where persons can reach beyond where they are?" (p. 100). In our work and our lives as educators and advocates we can take hold of these questions and use them to guide our reflection and our interactions in our everyday lives with our students, colleagues and others. Love, caring, criticality, hope and fighting are at the core of this work – these perspectives serve as the point for engaging the literature as well as praxis. Hope is a complementary color in this quilt; it blends the others together and gives the strength to continue. Critical pedagogy is more like the force, the needle that connects and moves the entire endeavor into action and bridges the gaps between theory and practice. Acting as the "bricoleur" (Kincheloe, 2007) I begin to piece these elements together into a cohesive whole, which presents a nuanced and multicolored picture of the ways in which criticality, advocacy, caring and armed love and hopeful practices in urban classrooms.

LENSES TO SEE, WAYS TO LEARN

Theoretical Framework and Methods

QUALITATIVE RESEARCH

When we choose our research, the questions that we ask not only reflect our interests, but also frame our methodological choices, and our designs (LeCompte & Preissle, 2003). As stated by Marshall and Rossman (2006), qualitative researchers do their work in naturalistic settings, and we are "intrigued by the complexity of social interactions expressed in daily life and by the meanings that the participants themselves attribute to these interactions" (p. 2). The purposes of qualitative research can be many, but among them, there is a motivation for advocacy research (Creswell, 2005) which recognizes the lack of political neutrality of research and instead harnesses it to work toward social change; this is particularly powerful. This is closely connected to the belief within critical pedagogical approaches of the importance of working toward social change at multiple levels.

Basing my work from this standpoint, I believe it is important to foster connections among university researchers and teacher-practitioners. This approach can be mutually enriching and creates space for dialogue and important changes within teaching and learning (Lagemann, 1999). One of the underlying goals of this approach is to challenge the traditional researcher-practitioner dichotomy that has structured the field. This continuing tension needs to be addressed in our research and our collaborative growth. As stated by Schensul and Berg (2004):

> When intellectuals not only reach outside of the university, but actually interact with the public beyond its walls, they overcome the ivory tower isolation that marks so much of current intellectual work. They create knowledge with those whom the knowledge serves. (p. 76)

Classrooms can become sites of powerful, transformative change by bringing together passionate and committed professionals in collaboration and co-creation of alternatives. My research is tied to these larger goals, as eloquently stated by Ayers (2006): "In our research, our teaching, and all our scholarly enterprises, our central goals include enlightenment and emancipation, human knowledge and human freedom" (p. 81).

Theoretical Framework

There are a variety of threads to weave together in the process of creating this quilt of research, and my theoretical framework draws on a variety of voices, lenses, and experiences to create the fabric. These standpoints allowed me to analyze my work with particular goals in mind for synthesis and analysis, and reminded me that there are multiple entry points into data. As stated by Schademan (2008), "social science researchers adopt theoretical frameworks in order to open their 'doors of perception.' They do so in order to derive meaning and gain insight from social phenomena" (p. 46).

Through the exploration of hope, love and praxis, I wanted to slightly change the discussion and perhaps the practices in schools serving non-dominant youth, practices which have historically been based on deficit discourses. This approach occurs in other places in the critical pedagogical world, where concepts of resource rich practices around marginalized youth and their families abound (see Akom, Cammarota & Ginwright, 2008; Ares, 2009; Duncan-Andrade & Morrell, 2008; Blackburn, 2005; Brayboy, 2005; Yosso, 2005; Solórzano & Delgado Bernal, 2001; Cammarota, 2007; Delgado Bernal, 2002; Schultz, 2007; Cammarota, 2004). While this is a sample of the literature focusing on strengths of marginalized youth, there is less literature regarding the strengths of teachers working with marginalized youth in a positive, political, powerful manner. This is a crucial omission, as we must focus on the interactions of teachers with their students if we hope to see change in everyday situations. With the larger educational discourse and system overly focused on standardization, testing and control, change must occur on the local level. Teachers' classrooms can offer this space of possibility. Of course there are some major works (Ladson-Billings, 1994; Nieto 2003, 2005; Darder, 2002) that do emphasize the importance of passionate, inspirational teachers, however only Darder's (2002, pp. 30–31) and Freire's works (2005, p. 74) center specifically on the concept of armed love or a pedagogy of love as important concepts for teachers. Darder states:

> We must come to recognize more concretely that living a pedagogy of love is intimately linked to our deep personal commitments to enter into relationships of solidarity with our students, parents and colleagues that support our humanity-namely our existence as full subjects within our world. But it cannot stop there! A pedagogy of love must encompass a deep political commitment to social justice and economic democracy. (2002, p. 89)

I chose to draw on caring and armed love (Noddings, 1984, 1992, 2002; Thompson, 1998; Darder, 2002; Valenzuela, 1999; Haskell McBee, 2007; Antrop-González & De Jesús, 2006; Freire, 1970, 1992, 2005) as well as critical pedagogy (Freire, 1970, 1998, 2005, Duncan Andrade & Morrell, 2008; Giroux, 1992; McLaren, 2003; Greene, 2003; hooks, 1994) to assist in the framing and development of this research.

My first lens incorporated the literature on caring, which was examined extensively in chapter 2. However, some of the points that are important for my theoretical framework include: the focus on supportive and nurturing relationships between teachers and students, and the ways that teachers conceive of and implement caring for their students. Authentic, caring connections between students and teachers are evident to students, and when they are missing, students suffer. As stated by Valenzuela (1999):

> an obvious limit to caring exists when teachers ask all students to care about school while many students ask to be cared for before they care about (school).

With students and school officials talking past each other, a mutual sense of alienation evolves. (p. 24)

True caring can be an antidote to this alienation. When we wrap ourselves and our students up in empowering, loving and critical relationships, I argue that we are nurturing and hence developing possibilities to change society. The ways that teachers perceive and enact caring are crucial to examine and understand more deeply. Caring and the ways it has been conceived of and discussed have been problematic, and the dangers of caring as based in whiteness, as belonging solely to "charity", condescension, and hierarchical concepts is a constant issue. How to balance out concepts of caring between that which is valuable and that which is condescending and Eurocentric, was one of the challenges.

My second theoretical choice is connected to caring, but takes on a distinctly political and social justice-oriented stance. It is a love based in struggle, solidarity and activism. Armed love is a complex concept to utilize as a theoretical lens, with a critical edge. It is connected to the work of Freire (2005) and Darder (2002) in the literature. However, other pieces show evidence of the concepts of armed love (Antrop-González & De Jésus, 2006; Rolón Dow, 2005; Schultz, 2007; Ware, 2006; Lynn, 2006; Beauboeuf-Lafontant, 2002; Ladson-Billings, 1994; Brown, 2009: Roberts, 2010) though they did not use this terminology specifically. For instance, Antrop-González and De Jesús focus on the practice of *critical care* within their research. They argue that it is through a continuum of *soft* and *hard* caring involving personal relationships and high expectations as well as genuine connections within the curriculum that support Latino/a students on multiple levels. Roberts (2010) articulates culturally relevant teacher caring as interconnected to the work of successful African American teachers. She argues that through this theoretical construct, African American teachers "feel a need to be vigilant in the fight against ongoing structural inequalities for African American youth and often demonstrate this dedication in their classrooms in unique ways" (p. 454). The concepts of struggle, "hard and soft", and fighting for students are reflective of the praxis of armed love.

Critical pedagogy, as my third lens, frames my work by asking deeper questions of the data about power and education, and the practices that I witnessed within my participants' classrooms. Freire (2007) argues:

I believe that, as progressive educators, we have the ethical responsibility to reveal situations of oppression. I believe it is our duty to create the means to understanding political and historical realities so as to bring about the possibility of change. (p. 3)

Through our work as teachers and researchers we can attempt to engage in praxis that helps this transformation to emerge. While the critiques are necessary, I argue that it is hope and *fighting love* which are also necessary components to engage practically in the world with its challenges. If teachers do not hold hope for their students, then what is in evidence in their practice? Hope is a foundational aspect of successful teaching, especially with students who have been marginalized.

It is important to consider within this research that I was interested in exploring both the conceptions of these important pieces, as well as their actualization in practice. Without the conceptual piece, actions could be non-reflective, and without the actions to support them, theoretical discussions can lack substance. The theoretical standpoints that I have mentioned here offer perspectives and possibilities to do this. The next sections will explore this more deeply. First, I will begin with a brief discussion of each of the frameworks, and then I will move to my methodological section.

Caring

> To speak of love in relation to teaching is already to engage in a dialogue that is taboo. When we speak of love and teaching, the connections that matter most are the relationship between teacher and subject taught, and the teacher-student relationship. Emotional connections tend to be suspect in a world where the mind is valued above all else, where the idea that one should be and can be objective is paramount. (hooks, 2003, p. 127)

Caring and love were examined in more detail in chapter 2, there are some distinct similarities, as well as differences. The famous work of Noddings (1984, 2002) brought caring into the discussion on education. As mentioned previously, this framework has some problematic aspects and was directly critiqued by Thompson (1998) for being Eurocentric. It was important to be rigorous in my examination of caring, and to check myself constantly that the definitions and manifestations that I witnessed were not based in a Eurocentric perspective. As a theoretical perspective, caring brings a deeper level of humanity into our educational interactions. It focuses on the emotional and interpersonal aspects of education, as based in our relationships and connections. Freire (1970) spoke of the importance of love for/with the oppressed as interconnected to struggles against the oppressors.

Armed Love

As stated by Darder (2002), discussing Freire's concept of love:

> I want to write about a political and radicalized form of love that is never about absolute consensus, or unconditional acceptance, or unceasing words of sweetness, or endless streams of hugs and kisses. Instead, it is a love that I experienced as unconstricted, rooted in a committed willingness to struggle persistently with purpose in our life and to intimately connect that purpose with what he called our true vocation'- to be human. (p. 34)

It is difficult to separate entirely the concepts of caring and armed love in the literature, and in fact they are closely related. However, as mentioned above by Darder (2002), armed love involves political commitment and struggle to create a more just world for our youth. Both caring and armed love are important to our youth, and this may be even more important for historically marginalized youth. There is a demanding aspect of this love that pushes youth to succeed despite tremendous challenges. Ladson-Billings' (1994) study touches on this issue, (though not this term specifically). The teachers in her research worked to critique society, as well as support and fight for the youth in their classrooms. In fact, much of the literature on caring argues that caring and love play a central role in improving or buffering the experiences of marginalized youth in schools (Valenzuela, 1999; Cassidy & Bates, 2005; Antrop-González & De Jesús, 2006). The creation of these spaces and how teachers practice and conceive of armed love for their students is of great importance.

With so much of our educational rhetoric focused on narrowly defined standards, we tend to forget the realities of students and teachers and the relationships between them. The classroom is interconnected to these relationships, and it is a potentially transformative space for building possibilities. Through my work, I wanted to bring caring and armed love to the forefront of the discussion, where it should be.

Critical Pedagogy

Critical pedagogy is connected to armed love. The reason for this is that teachers must have critical awareness to enact critical pedagogy. Wink (2005) talks about critical pedagogy as a "challenge to our assumptions" (p. 9). In playing this role, critical pedagogy allows us to change and grow as educators, as well as challenge our students' assumptions. Peterson (2003) argues that by transforming our educational spaces into more interactive and problem-to-solution focused places we can help enable our students to become critical seekers and questioners in their worlds, the potential for empowerment and awareness arise when critical approaches are engaged. Critical pedagogy helps us to look more deeply into our society and its institutions, and unearth the reasons why inequalities continue to thrive. The next steps involve working on collective ideas and projects about what to do about these injustices. The goals and ideals of critical pedagogy enable us to consider the dramatic potential for education toward democracy and social change. These are not new ideas, but the promise of equity and dreams of liberation still persist despite oppressive forces that operate to constrain them.

Critical pedagogy has a basis in the work of many intellectuals throughout the 20th century who engaged in critical traditions including; Gramsci, Foucault, Horkheimer, Adorno, Horton, Dewey, and more recently, Greene, hooks, Giroux, McLaren, Fine, Anyon and of course Freire (Darder, Baltodano & Torres, 2003). Because critical pedagogy "is fundamentally committed to the development and evolvement of a culture of schooling that supports the empowerment of culturally marginalized and economically disenfranchised students" (Darder, Baltodano & Torres, 2003, p. 11), it is germane to research and teaching within urban settings. Critical pedagogy allows us to critique our society through the very institutions which are problematic. In this case, teachers can act as conduits to different perspectives and forms of knowledge that encourage growth, understanding and activism within their students. Duncan-Andrade and Morrell (2008) point to the ways their work with students in schools is a form of developing " a counter-hegemonic education program" (p. 83). This was facilitated through focusing on criticality as well as personal factors such as self-respect and self-development in the students.

These different frameworks contribute to a mix of perspectives and analytical tools that coalesce to form a way of seeing teaching and schools that is both critical and yet retains hope. This is the benefit of drawing on these different, rich perspectives. It allowed me to view my data with more depth and, through various ways of knowing, I was able to "open up the spaces" and discover some powerful, beautiful points to enrich the discussion and to move toward change in education.

METHODOLOGY

Setting, Participants and Study Description

Setting

Rosa Parks High School (Parks) is a small, public high school, situated in a North-eastern US city, with a history of both radical social movements as well as racialized oppression. The city continues to struggle under the post-industrial and recession economy, and is sharply divided along the lines of race and class. This is evident in the ways the community understands the importance of location and space, in terms of one's class, wealth and schooling opportunities. It is commonly held "knowledge" that certain suburban schools are "good schools", while the city is frequently described as having "bad schools".

The school is a large red brick building, with an artistic awning supported by three pillars as you walk toward the entrance. It is located firmly downtown. The view of the school emerges quickly as you come around a wide curve, on the right hand side. There are parking lots, houses and a nearby commercial street surrounding the area, plenty of bus stops, and a couple of corner markets with flashing neon signs, too. There are also several excellent museums and it is not far from the theater and another urban school. My first day there it was dramatically windy, with shocks of blue sky and then dark gray clouds, as well as a sudden downpour that some of the kids got caught in. (They are allowed to leave school for lunch). There are several glass doors leading into a wide-open area with round tables, chairs, posters and flyers put up on the walls, and a small window where the security officer sells snacks and meals at lunchtime. The main office is to the left, with a small sign that denotes its place.

Participants

Two participants at Rosa Parks agreed to take part in my study. They were male veteran teachers, with 25 and 32 years of teaching experience respectively. They ranged in age from mid-50s to 60, and one participant was white and one was Black. They chose their pseudonyms as Clark Kent and Setshwayo Davis. They had both spent their entire teaching careers in urban settings, primarily in this particular district. They taught in different subject areas, one taught Social Studies, and one Math. They were both North-easterners. Each brought a distinctly different perspective to their understandings of love, praxis and critical pedagogy and teaching, which I will explore further when I elaborate on my discoveries.

Study Description

For deeper examination of the concepts of hope and radical love for urban teachers, instrumental case studies were a strong choice for the research. According to Stake (1995), cases can be instrumental or intrinsic in their basis, depending on the goals of the study. Intrinsic case studies are valued simply for the exploration of what is being studied, for instance as stated by Stake (2000), "I call a study an intrinsic case study if it is undertaken because first, and last, the researcher wants a better understanding of this particular case" (p. 437). The case itself is a worthwhile examination and research site for its own inherent value. Instrumental case studies, in contrast, are useful to understand larger concepts and ideas through the case study as a medium to do so. I was utilizing an instrumental case study to examine the concepts of hope, armed love and the praxis of transformative teachers. In-depth phenomenological interviews and videotaped classroom observation were my primary methods. The teachers were chosen through snowball sampling, with a maximum of 6 experienced, urban teachers as the original target number for participants. The study resulted in 2 participants total as mentioned, as 2 others were not able to participate as originally planned due to problems within the Central Educational Office, in terms of getting approval to access the other potential research site. Ethnicity/race for the teachers was not taken into account, but was self-described. However, one requirement that I stipulated was that they work within a district that is mostly composed of historically marginalized youth (African America, Native American, Latino/Hispanic -75% or higher). My participants also needed to meet a set of criteria as transformatively-focused educators, which centers on education as a political, liberatory act. These key concepts, such as a focus on the political aspects of education among other traits are mentioned in more detail below. The initial screening questions I asked of my potential participants were as follows:

- How do you see courage as related to your work/teaching?
- What do you think of the mission of teaching?
- How does social justice/compassion/love tie into your work?
- How is race/hope/activism a factor where (when?) you teach?

These questions were designed to help me ascertain my participants' standpoints and understandings of transformative teaching, which is drawn from a variety of literature. The elements that I wanted to screen for encompassed a wide range of traits. I was looking for traits such as a connection to social justice in education through a willingness and courage to "transgress" (hooks, 1994), the courage to question dominant norms and ways of knowing (Freire, 1998, Nieto, 2005), compassion for students (Haskell McBee, 2007), a strong belief in and passion for social justice (Nieto, 2005), an enthusiasm and commitment to education as transformative

(Darder, 2002, p. 92), awareness of caring as connected to activism (Beauboeuf-Lafontant (2005), a sense of teaching as a mission (Nieto, 2005), awareness of racialized/race based societal factors for urban youth, willingness to engage and challenge these in classroom space in a caring atmosphere (Cassidy & Bates, 2005), a revolutionary love (Duncan-Andrade & Morrell, 2008), and the importance of hope (Freire, 2004). This is an extensive list of traits, and I found that in the screening conversations, my participants touched on these elements at different levels. For instance, Clark spoke of challenging norms in schools and society as part of his teaching, but also the awareness that this may cause undesirable consequences. Setshwayo talked easily about race and his students' experiences, as well as the role of caring in his teaching. These themes were much more elaborated through the series of interviews that we did, and this range of traits helped me to create a very deeply nuanced portrait of the teachers' experiences and understandings.

Another important aspect for my research was that my participants be experienced teachers, with 10 or more years of experience in teaching, in order to provide a larger context for their knowledge and understanding of teaching, and to demonstrate that they have substantial information to draw upon in discussion. Many new teachers are grappling with their own teaching identity and juggling multiple roles and skills as they enter the profession. For example, Kauffman et al. (2002) found that new teachers struggled with creating and developing curricula and felt pressured by the many demands on them in their initial teaching experiences, including balancing student needs, classroom management, assessing and working with students, and covering material. Liston, Whitcomb and Burko (2006) echoed this, stating that studies have shown that stages of teacher development occur, with expertise manifesting only at the 4th year of teaching experience, or even later. I was much more focused on veteran teachers who have gotten to the point of comfort and use of intuition in the classroom, so they were able to focus on issues of social justice and equity within their classrooms, rather than focusing on the complex factors of professional identity and practice that newer teachers tend to struggle with. In order to recruit participants, I used my network of colleagues, professors and friends at the University, as well as my own experience and connections to certain teachers who work in the district. I first sent emails to my potential participants and then spoke with them by phone to give them an overview of what I was researching. The next step was to engage in a face-to-face discussion with my participants prior to initiating the research process and I shared with them my general topics and interests and described the interview and observation process for them. My own position as a researcher was a constant source of reflection for me in the establishment of relationships with participants in my research, including my whiteness, being a woman, being multi-classed and being connected to radical approaches in education. I made sure that I engaged in reflecting, journaling and analyzing my motives, intent, perceptions and writing during the research process. My greatest goal has been to describe the realities, wisdom and experiences of my participants, while respecting their standpoints, and presenting their ideas and worlds in ways that capture the realities as well as presenting them as alternatives to the predominant negativity in the discourse surrounding urban education.

DATA SOURCES AND DATA COLLECTION PROCEDURES.

My data sources were multiple and consisted of audiotaped and transcribed interviews, videotapes of classroom sessions, and field notes. For the videotapes of the classroom sessions, I began visiting the classrooms first without the camera, to begin to get familiar with my participants and the students. Then, I videotaped when I noticed that kids were becoming more comfortable with my presence. I began data collection in September of 2009, and continued collecting data until December, 2009. Though 4 months may not seem like substantial time, I was frequently in the school during this timeframe, between 2 and 4 days per week, for between 2 and 4 hours per day. In addition, the data I gathered within that time were incredibly rich. My data collection also coincided with the first half of the school year, from September until the December break.

For the interviews, my participants were interviewed in a 3-part series of individual sessions lasting approximately 1 ½- hours per session, which were digitally audiotaped, as well as the transcribed notes from our conversations. In my second interview with each participant, I utilized stimulated recall, using videotapes of their classroom teaching, to help gather their thoughts and perspectives on their own teaching, and to triangulate my data. According to Stake (2000), "Triangulation has been generally considered a process of using multiple perceptions to clarify meaning, verifying the repeatability of an observation of interpretation" (p. 443).

During the interviews, I recorded my data with a digital audio recorder, and then afterwards transcribed them in a word-for-word format. I included multiple periods to signify pauses, and sometimes included notes about facial expressions, tone of voice and emotional responses. Each interview focused on a slightly different aspect of participants' lives and experiences as teachers. For this, I was basing my work on the guidelines of Seidman (2006), with an in-depth phenomenological interview approach. The first interview was directed at obtaining the life history and background of participants, with the focus on what brought them to become teachers initially and asking them to recreate their own background and history. As stated by Seidman:

> In the first interview, the interviewer's task is to put the participant's experience
> in context by asking him or her to tell as much as possible about him or herself in
> the light of the topic up to the present time. (p. 17)

The second interview focused on participants' daily, lived experiences. For example, I asked them to talk about a typical class day, and what went on in the school on a weekly basis. The third and final interview was based on participants' perceptions and interpretations of the meaning of their experiences, drawing on the first and second interviews to surface themes and commonalities, such as how love and caring manifested in their classrooms and what they might connect between our interviews based on what we had spoken about. This provided a space for us to discuss what I had seen up until that point, and check with them to see if their interpretations were similar. Seidman (2006) refers to the purpose of the final interview: "Rather, it addresses the intellectual and emotional connections between the participants' work and life" (p. 18). Seidman argues for the importance of the three interview format. He states that by focusing on a specific aspect of participants' experiences, there is a logical format, and each session also lays the foundation for the next interview. I found this to be the case, as the interviews nicely complimented one another in the details, history and topics we discussed.

Data Analysis

For my analytic framework, I chose to use constructivist grounded theory (Charmaz, 2006), which involves close and careful approaches to our data corpus, and the generation of theories from what we find within it. I was looking specifically for emerging issues around participants' understandings of and implementation of armed love, caring and critical pedagogy, what they mean and how they manifest in their classroom practice. Through grounded theory analysis, I engaged in initial and then focused coding (Charmaz, 2006) to help in my search for ways teachers characterized and demonstrated armed love, hope and critical pedagogy. In terms of an approach to analysis, I used topical sets (Mehan, 1979). As stated by Mehan: "If the subtly woven process of classroom interaction is to be understood, rather than consider only the frequency of occurrence of single behaviors shown by teachers and students, one must examine sequential occurrences, multiple forms and simultaneous functions" (p. 27). For instance, the story that Clark told about metal detectors that were installed in the school was powerful. After coding this as an instance of despair, I went back through the data with this in mind. The despair aspect forced me to notice the tenuous nature of teaching in the city as perched between both hope and despair, and made me find other instances within the interviews which reflected despair. Through examination of the overall larger interactions, I was able to deepen my perception and understanding of hope, love and praxis in teachers' work, and the continuum of possibilities that can exist.

For my units of analysis, I chose cases, with the teachers being individual cases. Case studies are incredibly varied, and can consist of either an individual, or a setting or situation. Stake (2000) defines cases as specific, in-depth examinations of one particular situation/person/instance: "Custom has it that not everything is a case... The case is a specific One" (p. 436). In my research, the individual teachers and their teaching conceptions, environments, feelings and histories became the individual cases, which were investigated in detail. This was done in order to illuminate theoretical and practical dimensions of armed love, caring and critical pedagogy in keeping with the choice of an instrumental case study approach.

The recorded interviews were made into transcripts, and through examining these transcripts, I discovered themes and issues that were interesting and/or recurrent, related to armed love, pedagogy of love, and hope, as well as other themes that I had not anticipated before engaging in the work, such as understanding, community and certain aspects of spirituality. Stake terms this searching for "patterns and correspondences" (p.78). As the data gathering and analysis were very clearly an iterative process, there were times when I recorded, analyzed and interpreted, then reinterpreted the materials. Charmaz (2006) talks about the ways grounded theory researchers engage in initial coding, and then focused coding. She points to the fact that through initial coding, we are able to identify potential themes, and that the next step moves the process deeper, "you can begin focused coding to synthesize and explain larger segments of data" (p. 57). This next set of focused coding allowed me to look back through the 100 pages of transcripts and the approximately 25 hours of videotaped classes with an eye to the repeated themes that were strongly displayed.

I also used the videotaped classroom observations for analysis. For each participant, I observed them without taping for 1-2 sessions, just visiting their classes, and then I videotaped 7 classes per teacher, which lasted between 1 ½ and 2 hours per class. This was during their "Extended Class" time, from 1 – 2:30 or else 12:30 – 2:30. This happened in September, October, November and December, 2009. I used the Transana software system (www.transana.org) to code the data, and search for common themes, as well as create small clips of the data that were used in the second interview with participants, to stimulate reflection and discussion.

Researchers need to stay close to their data to avoid placing interpretations on the data that are not warranted. As a qualitative researcher, involving myself in the process of data collection and analysis, I was closely intertwined with my data. Stake (2000) speaks to the inherently evolving nature of case studies:

> Perhaps the simplest rule for method in qualitative casework is this: Place your best intellect into the thick of what is going on. The brain work ostensibly is observational, but, more basically, it is reflective… Qualitative case study is characterized by researchers spending extended time, on site, personally in contact with activities and operations of the case, reflecting, revising meanings of what is going on. (p. 445)

In this reflective and interpretive process, we need to pay close attention to the meanings, implications and underlying biases as connected to our positionality that can emerge within our research. I was consistently aware of this as I worked within the school, particularly my closeness to and yet my distance from the everyday activities, my privilege to come and go as I pleased, my lack of "accountability" to State standards, or schedules.

Sometimes I saw evidence that I was becoming part of the community, and yet I had the awareness that as a University researcher I was only partially connected, with duties elsewhere as well. My attempts to give back to the students and the school community were not always successful, and yet the determination that I brought with me to bring and share what I can persisted, whether it was knowledge, resources, suggestions, food, drink, or just a friendly interaction with the kids, letting them play with the video equipment.

Critiques have been directed at epistemological and methodological approaches that have not acknowledged or attended to the differing perspectives of people of color and women, essentially reinscribing "otherness" (Delgado Bernal, 1998; Fine, 1994; Harding, 1987; Daniel, 2005; Scheurich & Young, 1997). These were vital considerations as I sought to gain access to my site, engage in my research, interpret my data and work through the analysis process, not to mention negotiating the pull of classroom teaching and the realization that I genuinely do admire and adore teenagers. As a white, middle class woman involved in teaching, but not directly in the classroom, I needed to be aware of my assumptions. This was especially true for me regarding my sensitivity to issues of race and racism within classrooms. As I have focused much of my research on how racism is perpetuated in schools and what this looks like, it becomes incredibly easy for me to both see and focus on this issue. I needed to be aware and conscientious of my focus for this study, as well as reflective about my work. Researcher reflexivity is an issue that is mentioned previously by Stake (2000), and can be problematic within qualitative research. Fine, Weis, Weseen and Wong (2000) point to the tensions in including ourselves within the texts that depend greatly on the situated nature of the researcher her/himself. They argue that, "In the hands of relatively privileged researchers studying those whose experiences have been marginalized, the reflexive mode's potential to silence subjects is of particular concern" (p. 109). To assist with my own awareness and reflexivity, I was conscious of the importance of utilizing my colleagues and my participants to help in the interpretation process, in order to remain accountable and clear in my data analysis.

Ethical and Political considerations

The city that I live in is quite small and this was a primary ethical concern for me as a researcher. One reason had to do with maintaining confidentiality, and the other had to do with exiting the study gracefully and respectfully, remembering that we as researchers have certain status and power and need to be aware of how we are using it. For confidentiality and in order to protect my participants' privacy I needed to be careful with the recording of my data, as well as the documents that I produced from the data, and also in discussions with people on a casual basis, about my work and research. The interview data were recorded on a digital recorder and transcribed using my computer. When I engaged in transcribing the data, I used participants' initials, and when I moved to the actual writing, self-chosen pseudonyms of my participants were presented in order to maintain their privacy as well. I used only my laptop computer for this type of work, which is password-protected. I also kept my digital recorder in a locked filing cabinet in my home when I was not using it to obtain data. In addition to this, I discussed with my participants what to do to maintain their confidentiality, even while staying close to their meanings and perspectives. Within my research, participants, schools and the city were all given pseudonyms in the presentation of data.

Within the research we do it is important to acknowledge our own role as holders of a level of power, and our duties and responsibilities to our participants because of this. I found myself struggling so much with the weight of this, that in the beginning of the year, I did not want to enact my research.

The privilege, power and fear of becoming a "vulture" made me resist my own work. Pushing through my own resistance and keeping in mind the power and privilege aspects was a constant tension. As a qualitative researcher, I bring my opinions, experiences and positions to bear on my work, and I must be aware of the implications of this. This can be a challenge on multiple levels. In attempting to gain insight from the lives and understandings of others, qualitative researchers are close to their data emotionally, physically and mentally. This closeness can be a powerful way of connecting to our data, but can also be difficult as mentioned earlier, especially in relation to leaving the field site(s). Marshall and Rossman (2006) connect the importance of respecting our participants with our methods of exiting the data gathering situation: "Whether the researcher chooses to end the relationships, or to continue them in some way, being respectful of people and relationships is essential for being an ethical researcher" (p. 91). The authors also suggest that each researcher handles the level of connection to the participants after the study differently. I saw myself keeping in touch with them via occasional emails, in a friendly and informal manner, as well as stopping by to visit and chat. I wanted to maintain contact with both the kids as well as the teachers, because of the continual learning that I gain from this connection. I also wanted to keep a certain level of contact in order to find ways that I could continue to give back to the school community.

LOVING WITH A SWORD

Caring and Armed love in Clark and Setshwayo's Worlds

> It's hard to be a human being and deeply painful to be conscious…. To care, to love with every part of our wondrous selves, with the memory of every palpable cell of our beings. To reach out embracing life, in honor of all that is good, beautiful, sensual, just, brave, wise, funny. Yes, funny, in honor of life-giving humor. (Hernández-Ávila, 2002, p. 531)

In connection to the powerful quote above, conscious caring *hurts* as much as it heals. I came into this research with the perspective that these powerful emotions and actions are taking place within our urban schools, and they don't receive enough emphasis in our conceptions and representations of teachers and teaching, in either research or in practice. My focuses on armed love, caring, hope and critical pedagogy were intertwined as well as complicated, as instances of hope and despair emerged pointing to the pain as well as the healing.

It becomes difficult to frame everything into a "neat" or even vaguely linear story. Critical pedagogy surfaced in the teachers' practice, and caring and armed love were demonstrated in many different facets of practice and understanding. Because of this, the process of becoming a *bricoleur* (Denzin & Lincoln, 2000) became critical in assembling my research. Utilizing the quilting analogy, when I began to explore my findings it seemed that there were masses of fabric, scraps, string and patterns that could be brought together and yet only one quilt was to be made. In addition to this, some things are difficult to surface, and even more difficult to write about when they come from the deep, emotional places in our hearts and souls. I learned at multiple levels, and I also discovered that people's experiences are richer and more complex than we often understand. There are so many myths, misconceptions and forms of violence that urban kids are put through, and when looking at our wealthy and privileged society, these issues are simply tragic and incredibly unfair, a modern manifestation of Jim Crow legacies. Since when (since always?) has a child's zip code determined her human rights?

Through this chapter, I will delve into what emerged from the data. I will give a description of each of the participants and the school, and then deeply explore and bring the main themes back into connection with the literature. Returning to the quilt metaphor, I found it to be visually rich and deep, and in presenting it, I hope that the beauty and intricacy of this creation can mirror that of the actual experience.

School

Rosa Parks School (Parks) began in 1971 as an alternative school, and originated in the beliefs and hard work of a group of teachers, parents and students. As stated by Foote (2009) who examined the history of the school in connection to standardized testing through her dissertation:

> These teachers, witness to violent school riots at Livingston (another CSD school), believed that many of the problems in their school could be traced to the institution of schooling itself: its rigid structure of segregated subjects dictated by the state, taught in enclosed classrooms in isolated periods of approximately 42 minutes each, with the entire system monitored by a hierarchy of teachers and administrators. Inspired as well by the 'de-schooling' atmosphere of the late 1960s and early 1970s, this cadre of teachers - a distinct minority at Livingston - wanted to break down these artificial 'walls' and develop a different kind of learning environment: one in which students, under the guidance of adults, would learn how to become independent learners by pursuing issues and topics of their own interest in real-life settings throughout the community, and by making decisions with staff on how to develop and run their school. (p. 56)

Since it originated, there have been periods of relative calm and also periods of upheaval in relation to the District and State mandates about standardized testing. Struggles against standardized testing, budgets, and also questions of mission and adherence to the basic philosophy of the school have been a part of its development since early on (Foote, 2009). The participants that I worked with also touched on some of these instances, including the sentiment that the kids have changed, the school has changed, the style of the administration has changed, and that these changes are not necessarily in a positive direction. In contrast to this, my interactions with the school and the students were overwhelmingly positive, and I felt that there were complexities that, as a visitor, I could not always grasp, but also as an outsider, that I had a fresh perspective on what I saw during my observations, videotaping and interviews. I believe I was able to see both the strong points and the potential weak points within the school community.

Below, I have brought together narrative stories about each of the participants. These were compiled based on both formal and informal conversations, including the first life-history interviews with each participant. Interestingly, they chose very different pseudonyms, which reflect something of each of their characters and perspectives, and will also give the reader a sense of the specialness of each.

CLARK KENT

Clark Kent is a white man in his 50s, with small glasses; he is completely bald and very energetic, with deliberate, quick movements. He seems incredibly focused in the moment, judging by the deep interactions he has with the kids and also with me. He wears jeans, sweatshirts and sporty shoes to class, and leads an afternoon yoga session with his extended class every day. He is also an excellent cook and is fortunate to have a full kitchen in his classroom. In our first interview, he told stories of his past that help me to understand his background, and how he came to teaching, which he has been doing now for 32 years, in urban settings in two different North-eastern states. This interview helped me to understand more of the nuances of his past, and challenged some of my ideas about how those who are exemplary teachers end up in education.

I began by asking him how he came to be a teacher, and it was an indirect route to the classroom to say the least. In high-school, he was very highly placed within his class, and when he spoke to the guidance counselor about wanting to be a teacher, he says, "I was told I had 'too much potential, so I was a pre-med major". I also asked him if his family supported his decision to become a teacher and he said that even though his Mom was an elementary school teacher:

> No, they didn't… Well, I had "more potential".. now once I became a teacher, they were supportive – but it was interesting – probably up until like 10 years ago – they thought I would be going into administration, or getting a Ph –which I did start, after several PhD starting, I just… I, I didn't have the political stamina to be in Higher Ed…

His undergraduate major was in math and physics, and after college he taught as a substitute teacher for a while, and then worked at a gourmet shop. He decided to go to Colorado, and focus on studying plant genetics. This department presented some challenges for him, and he ended up changing direction and heading back East to Penn State:

> I ended up.. back at Penn State, and a major in economics and a minor in nutrition. I majored in Home Ec. (Interruption from kid) Ummm. So it was more, economics and nutrition, and at Penn State, it was fairly…. they were active…

He described the progressive nature of the program, including his role as a graduate assistant in 1975, which included scanning and removing texts for gender bias, and an openness and progressive stance toward presenting important and difficult topics such as sex education. He was also the first male home economics teacher in our North-eastern State, ever:

> When I started… I liked learning.. and one of the things that I realized in the course of the Penn State teacher ed. Program, well the Home Ec. Program, that it was so much about thinking and learning and reflection, that I realized that teaching is about constant reflection and learning – that even in the subject areas you are always refining, you're reflecting on what you're gonna do with the kids, and I realized that it wasn't something that I was going to get bored with. That was something that I realized earlier on– other things where I switched my majors that I started thinking I was getting bored…

Even though there were several different paths that he tried, teaching seems to be a space that he could situate himself in more comfortably. As mentioned above, there is something about the constantly changing learning and reflecting that teachers engage in which sparked his interest in teaching as a career. Clark was very specific though, that high school kids are his ideal age group to work with – he laughed and seemed a bit overwhelmed (even in memory) of working with an elementary-aged population, with his shrug and eye-rolling combining to tell me that the younger ones were not for him. He found out after substitute teaching that teenagers suited his style and interactions more completely. He entered the profession as the first male home economics teacher in our State. He began at an urban middle school, taught there for a year, moved into the district office as a nutritionist for the district, and then went back to the classroom, always within our urban district. Overall, he spent

13 years in different schools, and then came to Parks 19 years ago and has been there since then. He continues to teach, and talks about teaching as inspiring him to laugh on a daily basis, and also having the power to depress him with the challenges of administration, kids that he can't quite reach, and standardized tests. The class that I observed with him was a journalism class, during the school's "Extended Class" time, from 1:00 to 2:30 pm, or 12:30 to 2:30 on Tuesdays.

SETSHWAYO DAVIS

Setshwayo Davis (this name comes from the last Zulu king, overthrown by the British) is an African American man who is 60 years old; he laughs and smiles brilliantly. I felt an immediate connection with him when I met him, and he seems to radiate a level of peace, patience and wisdom that I have seldom seen. He generally wears dress pants and sweaters to school, and has dark hair that is tinged with silver. Both his ears are pierced and he often has small studs in them. He began teaching at a later age than most enter the profession, and he came into teaching in a very unique and indirect way as well. Setshwayo was the third person in his family to get a college education. He went to college intending to major in business, specifically in marketing. He talks about the ways that teachers were consistently influential in his life, even though he initially chose a different path:

> (*I*) Followed that mantra, go into business, go where the money is, but I still had this tremendous respect for teachers, and over the years, I would stay in touch with some of my teachers, in fact one of my good friends in junior college, his brother was my Math teacher in high school, in fact he was the only African American on staff, and he was my track coach, and he was like the big brother I didn't have...

That path toward the world of business and marketing was disrupted, however, when he was drafted into the military. Setshwayo served two years in the army, and returned to the States with a different perspective:

> I really didn't decide on teaching, I got drafted, went to Vietnam, and, someone asked me the other day... I think it was Hassan – what did you want to take in college at first, I said I was a business major – he said "Aw man, if you had stayed that, man you'd be livin' large, you'd have a Mercedes..." I said "Yeah that's possibly the way it'd go", I said, "but something, things happen to you in your life's journey", I said, the thing that really, made me question this whole drive towards business was my experience in Vietnam, when I got back from the service, I was gone for 2 years, spent a year in Vietnam, I didn't know what I wanted to do, so I went to work at (Mega-Corporation) for 3 years, and um, I think those 3 years at Mega-Corporation really turned me off to the business world.

When he felt conflicted about continuing in the business world, he actually phoned a former teacher who advised him that perhaps he wanted a career that was more meaningful, and would provide a way for him to give back to others. Setshwayo left the business world and returned to finish his college education at the age of 24. After he finished his Bachelor's degree he worked as a teacher at a community organization that assisted kids in need. After several years, he decided to return to school to finish his teaching credentials, and he began by substitute teaching throughout the city school district. It was at this point that, as he says, "This is for me, I really like teaching". He worked for 6 years teaching at a middle school, and was invited to teach at Parks in 1986, and has been there ever since, as a Social Studies teacher. The class that I observed with him was entitled "Activism", and plays dual roles as both focusing on English and Social Studies, during the Extended Class time. The Extended Class session of the day goes from 12:30-2:30 or 1:00-2:30 every afternoon except Thursdays. The teacher acts as an advisor for all students within his or her Extended Class, and there is a special, familial atmosphere in the Extended Classes.

Caring/Armed Love

> I think you also have to love the kids... and genuinely love them.

I discovered that both caring and armed love were prevalent in my participants' worlds, conceptually and in practice. The prevalence of caring and armed love were also evident in the literature, and these concepts can take on a wide range of approaches and definitions. Valenzuela (1999) placed caring in a cultural context, and examined the ways it was demonstrated (and lacking) at her research site. In her work, she pointed to the multiple challenges that teachers and students faced when attempting to achieve authentic caring. In my research, I found that authentic caring was demonstrated by teachers through their connections with the kids. These were genuine connections, which involved a spectrum of interactions from playful, to serious, to authoritarian, to mentor. Clark mentioned the fact that there was a definite strictness necessary with his students, but also a level of playfulness as well. I also discovered caring and armed love are intricately interwoven. Originally I had separated these sections, but on further investigation (and with the help of my advisor) we determined that in fact caring and armed love are complementary. They are manifestations of the ways that teachers nourish, support and love their students, as well as challenge them. The demonstration of these elements in practice is explored further within the next section.

Caring

Clark defined caring:

> I think caring, so caring is giving them the time and attention. Umm, listening... and the food, yeah, so like in the Fall I'll have fruit here all Fall, in the winter if I can find stuff reasonably, I will. I cook for them twice a week, on their birthdays, I make for the class, whatever they've requested that I make...

Food was an especially noticeable component of Clark's work with (and nurturance of) the kids. As an excellent cook, he also recognized the importance of food in building community and creating a social atmosphere.

On a day in November, when I entered the classroom, it was thick with smoke, and the scent of sausages, pancakes and bacon. The kids were making a brunch to share with one another. During this particular day, the kids enjoyed Stromboli, French toast, juice, two kinds of bacon, eggs, grits, and hash browns. After the brunch was ready and the kids had helped themselves, Clark walked around with a small bag of cheese offering it to the kids for their grits. While the kids ate, Clark took the time to thank them individually for their cooking contributions to the feast. Another instance from my field notes captures a snippet of the classroom interactions in terms of caring as well:

> Kids engage in important and interesting discussions – torture, border patrols, etc... kids are funny, the kids seem a little animated today!!! There is so much laughter in the room – lots of little comments and such, CK quiets class – then offers chocolate cake, in nice square slices on brown paper towels. Kids get up and go and eat, sit down. I get some cake too.

There was laughter, eating and critical discussions occurring simultaneously here. The caring and sense of community were evident in the comfortable atmosphere, and interactions. For the holidays, the students bring in dishes to share as well, and during one class I saw them choosing what they would like to bring in for Thanksgiving. The result was a feast with a wide variety of dishes that both Clark and the kids cooked. In the time that I was there, I also enjoyed some of the more "everyday" food, like pasta and curried lentils, which he routinely cooks 2-3 times per week for the kids. During our interviews, he mentioned food as important as an aspect of modeling behavior, and as a community-builder. In our second interview he stated, "Well, I think modeling is probably the most powerful teaching tool. It's why I do the things like bringing in the food, with the idea that they'll... reflect that". When I asked Clark about kids' responses to the food, he mentioned that he sees them bringing food in and sharing with the group as well. He also said that they get to choose anything they would like for their birthdays, and he will make it for them. As an example of this, he spoke of the ways that when he makes brownies, he needs to make them half with nuts and half without, because some of the kids like nuts, while others don't. This attention to detail of what the kids like or don't like is an excellent example of a small but significant demonstration of caring.

In addition to food, Clark also explicitly spoke about teaching as being closely interconnected to relationships. I noticed both within the video excerpts as well as in our interviews that Clark talked about the necessity of paying individual attention to the kids. One day, a student entered late and he looked at her and said, "Thank God you're here, I was gonna cry", the girl answers "You was gonna cry?" and Clark says "Yes, because you weren't here, by the way, I like your hair like that". This short interaction demonstrates the ways that Clark notices the kids, and addresses them in a playful and friendly manner. He talked about the fact that kids really need this kind of genuine attention, and he feels that supplying it is an important aspect of caring: "Time is a precious commodity and I think one of the things that... like giving them your undivided attention and time... that's something, I'm not sure how used.. they are to it, but they *need* it".

He also mentioned the importance of honesty with youth, demonstrating recognition that this serves to establish both relationship and trust: "when I said about being genuine… when you love the kids, and caring about them, if you're honest with them all the time, they're more likely to listen". He spoke about this in reference to the fact that one of his first classes involved teaching nutrition to a group of kids who were involved with drugs. His point through our conversation focused on the fact that he felt that if he told kids that all drugs were equally damaging, he would be dishonest with them. Instead he chose to focus on the different effects of drugs on the body and its ability to retain nutrition, differentiating between the dangerous forms of drugs and the less serious ones. This aspect of honesty and understanding the kids' lives was a prevalent theme in Clark's work.

Community in the classroom was also important to Clark, and he saw this as being connected to the quality of relationships established:

> My belief is, every single student should feel secure in a classroom, that they should feel… they should feel like it's a community. That they can be themselves, that they can share, and that no one is going to criticize them for that or make fun of them.

He referred to the classroom community frequently, and at one point talked about it like a "sphere" that had the potential for maintaining a sense of balance and consistency. He pointed to the ways the classroom could function well, despite outside factors that may be ineffective or even destructive in the kids' lives.

Caring in Clark's classroom emerged as a connection to his values as well:

> There's certain things in my classroom, you live by my values, that's the political, I hope they'll take those and use them when they interact with other people.. you know, caring, sharing, giving, being non-violent, uhh… thinking, analyzing, critiquing, but doing it in such a way as to… not threaten anyone.

Clark mentioned that his strong belief in the power of modeling was one way that he helped to bring these values into his work. Incorporating these values into his classroom, Clark worked to enable the kids to create a cohesive and caring community.

For Setshwayo, caring was also represented through his conception of the Extended Class in particular as a community, (which he referred to several times as like a family) and in his demonstrations of affection and support for the kids. Several times when I visited, they were planning celebrations together (Thanksgiving and Christmas) and in fact Setshwayo gently chastised me for missing the Thanksgiving celebration because of one particular activity which involved the group getting together, holding hands, and sharing what they were thankful for. He spoke with pride and affection of the honesty, thoughtfulness and insight of his students' sharing in a community setting. This is a difficult scenario to imagine in many "mainstream" schools, and shows openness and caring within the classroom atmosphere among the students.

In another case, Setshwayo discussed the close connection to his students differently. One painful and powerful example of this happened around the time of our second interview, about a very serious health issue that one of his students may be facing:

> When I see kids who are not their normal self, I will ask them – "Is everything ok, is there anything I can do?" Young lady shared with me that she might have cancer, my response was to embrace her, and hold her and tell her to pray and listen to her doctors, and if there was anything I could do for her, to come to me, and I'd help her, there's that real nurturing side of me that father, big brother.

I could see the intense emotions here, as well as the importance of knowing the kids and understanding their worlds and needs, even when they are difficult and sad. In this particular instance, the realization and deep understanding of his students' suffering was obvious in our discussion. His voice became quiet, and his eyes were full of seriousness when he described this interaction. This deep connection is an integral part of teaching, according to him. When the student asked him about the work she needed to make up, and the ways she could meet the assignment requirements, he told her that the most important thing now in her life was taking care of herself and listening to her doctor. He showed his awareness of the human elements of teaching, and the necessity for caring, especially in this challenging situation. In our first interview he said, "You can't be in this profession and not be a care-giver, you can, but you're doing a lot of faking". He also implied that the kids would be able to see through any "fake" caring that a teacher presents.

The realization that a connection and understanding of the kids was crucial was expressed during our interview sessions. Setshwayo mentioned that he strikes a balance with the kids, of insisting that they complete their work well and in a timely fashion, but that he also discusses a wide range of issues and offers support to them during their "conference" times, which are 22 minute, one-on-one sessions with each of the kids in his extended class, during lunchtimes. He expressed the fact that this individual time was a space for creating connections and relationships with the students, and also gives them a place to discuss whatever they would like, both academic and non-academic topics:

> I think here too, we have conferences with kids, and that way you can have a personal dialogue with them, about what's working and what's not working and things that you can point to them that could help them along the way, and in a more traditional school, you don't have that time or space, you know, that's left up to the guidance counselors, and the guidance counselors have 3, 4, 500 kids, you really don't, you might be able to affect, half a percent, but here with that personal relationship you can have with kids, I think you'd have a much better chance, of, of, giving them a different path, opening up a door.

This theme surfaced in Cassidy and Bates (2005), where the authors mentioned the centrality of these connections and relationships with kids, and argued that by taking on multiple roles of mentor, care-giver and teacher, the atmosphere contributed to allowing them to "be there" for their students and to get to know them as whole people (p. 83).

Clark spoke of the importance of the conferences as something that was important as well as special within this school. He described conferences as "powerful" and laughed when mentioning the fact that he still has (former) students who return on a regular basis to conference with him. He commented that some of these former students are even 24 years old. In Antrop-González and De Jesús' (2006) work, they mentioned:

Student informants from both schools described experiences of educational caring linked to high academic expectations and mentorship as central features. These reported experiences highlighted an emphasis on high-quality interpersonal relationships at the two schools. (p. 421)

This kind of caring relationship involves the teachers' willingness to be genuine with the students, and to allow themselves to be whole people as well. Setshwayo was direct and honest with his class, and shared his own humanity, both strengths and weaknesses with the kids. In fact, one of the videotaped sessions that I was involved in was so delicate and difficult that I wondered whether I should shut the camera off, and sincerely debated including it within this work. It seemed incredibly important though, and is a testament to the character and honesty that Setshwayo demonstrated as a teacher. In late November, during the second class that I videotaped, Setshwayo shared that he was a survivor of cancer. This particular session was one that touched me deeply, and taught me about the power of his honesty and relationships with the kids, that he would show them something that was so personal and clearly life-changing for him. It was also incredibly human, a reminder of the difficulties and challenges that people face. This was an example of the undercurrents of sadness that can occur, despite our inability to see these issues on the surface. These life-changing realities are part of our everyday worlds, and our vulnerability as well as our strengths. In our second interview, we spoke a bit about this, and he mentioned that it is something he chose to share for the first time with a class this year, and that it depended very much on the dynamics of the group, as well as his personal realizations of what it means to be a survivor. I believe the respect that I saw the kids presenting (as demonstrated by their careful listening and words of surprise when Setshwayo told them, and also a show of seriousness and maturity in their responses) was based partly on the ways that he was extremely sincere with them, and cared enough to share the multiple facets of himself.

Setshwayo also plays with his students. At the school, each of the extended class teachers is responsible to do some gym-type activity with their students once a week. Setshwayo takes his class to a local community recreation center, where they play basketball, kickball or volleyball. One class that I videotaped involved a gym session, where the kids formed teams and played kickball and volleyball. This non-traditional form of engagement with the kids is a powerful way to present multiple facets of oneself as a teacher, and it's clearly fun for the kids as well. By non-traditional, I mean the ways that a social studies teacher played another role within the school, that of gym teacher. In most schools, there is a strict division by individuals in the roles and subject areas in which they work with youth. In this case, the social studies teacher shifts into a different role every Monday afternoon and becomes like a coach instead of solely a classroom teacher. Also, he switches to playing with them, rather than directing or guiding them in the classroom, this is an additional facet of their interactions. It was also interesting that during this particular episode, there was a verbal fight between a girl and a boy in the class, over her scoring out during kickball. The girl approached the boy and began yelling loudly at him.

Setshwayo handled this in an interesting way, not overreacting, but clearly addressing the situation respectfully and authoritatively with the students. He addressed the girl, "Asia, Asia, Asia, *Asia*! Do you want to spend the rest of the time outside? Close your mouth." Then he turned and walked back to his position as referee on the field. There was a clear show of authority that remained caring and not destructive within this interaction. He handled the crisis without sacrificing or compromising his connection with either youth. He was confident in his connection to the student, that she would listen to him, and she did. Asia stepped out to the bathroom then came back into the gym more composed the game continued on.

Despite this incident, the rest of the class went smoothly. I noticed kids shouting when they scored, dancing and even clapping and gently teasing one another as well. There is a level of comfort and care in evidence in their interactions, by the informality and playful atmosphere among the group. The kids were wholeheartedly participating, and Setshwayo helped facilitate their game as referee.

Howard (2001) found this holistic approach important in creating genuine relationships with students, understanding that we are multifaceted beings. Noddings' work, cited in Valenzuela (1999), states that for caring to be effective, there needs to be engagement from the teacher and the willingness to start a connection, "with engrossment in the student's welfare following from this search for connection... When the *cared-for* individual responds by demonstrating a willingess to reveal her/his essential self, the reciprocal relation is complete" (p. 21). By presenting himself as a complex human being, Setshwayo was initiating this form of connection, allowing space for authentic caring to emerge.

In terms of caring specifically, Setshwayo spoke of the necessity of being connected to the kids in order to be within the teaching profession. This was something that he learned early on from his first teachers, as well as his later mentors, the importance of connection:

> you know, you don't love 'em all, some, you care about more than others, but you try to connect, even the ones who are a pain in the ass – you let 'em know – "You don't have to be like this... So even kids who you don't connect with, there's a way to let them know that you care about what they're doing, and that what you see of how they're operating in the world... it's not creating positive energy. I have not known <u>any</u> teachers, well, I can't say that – there's been a few people, at the end of their career, where it's obvious they're putting their time in – maybe they shoulda retired a few years earlier, you know, but for the most part, most of the teachers I've known have been really caring people, and I have been very blessed with that.

Clark approached caring slightly differently. He focused on modeling behaviors for the kids as a demonstration of caring and connection, in the hopes that these behaviors would be learned through this. Through this technique, he hoped that he is showing what he would like them to apply in the classroom as well. One instance of this from the videotaped classroom sessions was noticeable to me when two of the kids were leading a whole-class discussion, and Clark stepped off to the side of the classroom to listen respectfully and allow the two youth to take over in his stead. During the discussion, the expectation of raising one's hand was also played out by Clark, modeling respect for the speakers and willingness to wait his turn to speak. He was also demonstrating his own ability to adhere to the classroom rules and norms, even as the teacher. In addition, he was demonstrating that caring involved his participation in the group as an equal, rather than a "superior". He would raise his hand and wait to be called on by the students, in an interesting reversal of the traditional space and power in classroom settings, where the teacher tends to be quite directive.

Both participants touched on the ways that creating a group that was close, honest and cohesive influenced the success of kids' sense of belonging and learning in the classroom, and connected this to the special atmosphere of their classrooms and the school. The importance of relationship building, care and love was a repeated theme within the research literature as well (Antrop-González & De Jesús, 2006; Cassidy & Bates, 2005; Van Sickle, 1996; Noddings, 1984, 1992; Haskell McBee, 2007; Valenzuela, 1999; Ware, 2006; Howard, 2001; Ladson-Billlings, 1994; Lipman, 1995). A necessary ingredient in all of these classrooms was love. This is not the simple or overused cliché of love, but a deeper and powerfully dedicated form of caring. This caring is dedicated to a larger social project, and simultaneously based in individual relationships with the kids.

In the next section I will elaborate on the facets of caring through armed love. The following section explores instances of armed love that I encountered with my participants, a love that involves a distinctive political awareness and advocacy for historically marginalized youth.

ARMED LOVE

Demanding and Understanding

Armed love differed slightly from caring. It extended caring into a form of advocacy and struggle for students' lives and best interests. One of the manifestations of armed love that I witnessed revolved around demanding social responsibility while maintaining a deep understanding of the difficulties confronting the students. This involves a political awareness of the realities that many urban students face, as well as the willingness to fight against this. This form of interconnection contrasts with some horrifying environments that urban youth can be subjected to, which may involve teachers and schools in which domination, militaristic control and dehumanization are the norm (Alonso, Anderson, Su & Theoharis, 2009; Monahan, 2009; Valenzuela, 1999; Kozol, 2005). Having visited urban schools where passing through metal detectors, and encountering the concepts of the attributed "criminality" of students, it is crucial that we investigate spaces where individuals fight against this. This is where armed love plays a vital role as both counterstory and antidote.

There was a clearly demanding aspect of their teaching in spite of (or because of) the challenges kids face, which was always mindful of the challenges. For instance, in our first interview, Setshwayo stated his role with the students:

> it's really, being uh, someone who gives them the ability to understand their options in life and what their potential is. Um, I had a conference with one of my kids today, who earned very little or no credit and she's a very affable, gregarious young girl and she's got great potential, but she's squandering it, and I said "You know something, you got great potential, but it's very frustrating to see you just not do anything with it".

In this instance, Setshwayo was warning her about the pitfalls of "squandering her potential", as well as pushing her to do better. He is acting with understanding and compassion, while also challenging this student to become something more in line with the potential which he can see within her.

For Clark, understanding kids and demanding certain behaviors were interconnected. They emerged from the armed love which he engages in his classroom. He stated:

> I sometimes see it, when a kid's behavior is wrong and instead of letting them know clearly that the behavior is wrong, the teacher will talk to them and go over things, and there's a difference between understanding where a kid comes from, you can understand that, but that doesn't mean the behavior is correct.

By compassionately recognizing students' motivation, but also setting the guidelines for responsibility he balances these facets out effectively.

Setshwayo also spoke of his willingness to be there and support the kids, and to help them navigate their issues. There was also the simultaneous necessity to speak honestly about their shortcomings, and to warn them of the potentially dangerous consequences to their lives:

> (*I*) tell 'em, "You're much better than this" "You are bright, but your priority of doing well in school is not there, your priority is hanging out and having a good time, and you're gonna run out of time, ok, you don't wanna be graduating from high school at age 20, and that's the path that you're on".

His wisdom and experience contributed to the insights which he could provide for the students. In the example above, there is the understanding of this youth's choices and priorities, while also asking her to take the necessary time to think through her choices more clearly.

Setshwayo showed insistence and persistence by supporting students through the difficulties and demanding they meet the challenges. He said in an interview that he believed this directness was critical to youth's success both in high school and the larger world:

> ok, I'm 'onna put it right in your face, "You did not do well and there's no reason for it. You know what I see you doin' I see you bein' lazy, irresponsible, mkay,(*sic*) not usin' your time wisely"... I tell the kids all the time, "What you do here in high school has a lot to do with what you're gonna do in the rest of your life, you may not believe it, but believe me when I tell you, I'm sure there's some things that I coulda done a whole lot better in high school, and I wish I had.

Students' lives are powerfully impacted by the social constraints that surround them. Examples such as the poverty that is insidious in the city and the fact that good job opportunities are scarce are contributing factors. There are also strong elements of racial/class segregation, under-funding of both the community and its educational facilities and alternative economies such as drugs which continue to haunt the city. Students may have complicated family situations, or be responsible for themselves. By being aware, loving and demanding in the face of these challenges, my participants acted as advocates and warriors for their students and they showed armed love for them.

Clarity and High Expectations

High expectations for academics, as well as authority played a strong role in the demonstration of armed love. Clark was also clear that armed love includes honesty and directness with kids about what the expectations are for the classroom, and their behavior. The importance of clarity, combined with direct communication of high expectations, were other facets of armed love. Both Clark and Setshwayo touched on the ways which clear and direct communication about academic responsibilities were crucial.

Setshwayo stated that his directness and unwillingness to let kids fail were a part of his "tough love" for them. Clark was also very concise when explaining the fact that telling a kid when he/she is doing something unacceptable is an aspect of caring for the kids, and that it is not only about being liked by the students, "I think some teachers make the mistake of thinking that if... if they say no, or if they...don't put... restrictions that kids won't like them". Clark emphasized in this statement that creating boundaries and expectations are both involved in armed love, that through the boundaries armed love and caring are actively displayed. This demonstration of authority communicates to youth that their teachers care enough to push them, and expect better of them when they don't do well. It also points to the importance of communication with students about their roles and responsibilities, while simultaneously encouraging them to meet these expectations. There is a combination of belief, expectation and directness found within these practices.

This is echoed elsewhere in the literature on teachers, authority and high expectations (Brown, 2009; Antrop González & De Jésus, 2006; Darder, 2003; Bizell, 1991; Noblit, 1993; Siddle Walker, 2000; Foster, 1997). Many times research has shown that successful educators of historically marginalized youth understand the necessity of high expectations for their students (Foster, 1997; Ladson-Billings, 1994). In fact, this is also tied closely to the continual struggle against marginalization and racism, and education has been a deeply held commitment in the Black community as a means of empowerment and racial uplift (Siddle-Walker, 2000). The work of Darder (2003) and Brown (2009) speak specifically to pedagogies of caring as deeply connected to authority and highly demanding expectations of youth. Within Darder's work, she highlighted exemplary educators who engage in the continual work to "reinvent" Freirean approaches and connect to critical, caring pedagogies. She states that "teachers must critically utilize their power in the interest of democratic life or '*on the side of freedom*' [Freire 1998c, 74] to authorize dialogical conditions in the classroom" (p. 111, emphasis original).

Brown's work highlights African American male teachers' pedagogical performances, one of which is "The enforcer". In this instance teachers demand discipline and order, while demonstrating for youth that their expectations are set high and young people are anticipated to meet them. Siddle Walker's (2000) work explicitly examines common themes within segregated schools from 1935-1969. She found "exemplary teachers" who were "consistently known for their high expectations for student success" (p. 264).

Bizell's (1991) work touches on the many complexities of enacting critical pedagogies and their implications in the classroom in connection to authority. Bizell argues toward the end of her piece that authority is absolutely necessary when enacting progressive education in the classroom, when it is in the direct interests of the students. Teacher authority and expectations combine to create an environment where students may not simply hide and "slip by".

Setshwayo told a story of a student approaching him years ago, and asking if he was Mr. Davis, when he said yes, the student said, "You don't take nothin' from nobody" in a tone of respect and admiration, and then asked if he could join his class. Both Clark and Setshwayo stated and demonstrated that high expectations of the kids' behavior and academics were connected to their dedication to the kids, and that this was a part of their role and responsibility as teachers. Clark was very specific about both the importance of expectations, and the necessity to have high expectations combined with the willingness to tailor them to the situation and the student:

> Well my expectation is that every kid do every assignment and do it to the best of their ability. I also recognize that every kid has a different ability level, so my expectation for one student, my expectations for all of them are the same, as far as doing the work, and how much they do. My... understanding is... especially in a heterogeneous group that kids come in with different ability levels... I have high expectations, I expect all kids to do work, um,, I have... a very defined work ethic. I expect kids to develop a work ethic because in my... my belief... and in my observations, the kids, people with good work ethics will always succeed.

Clark very clearly stated to the kids what was due, and on what days, and then what the consequences would be if something was not handed in. He wrote the dates and assignments due in the upcoming two weeks on the overhead, and then reviewed what the expectations were for the kids for each assignment. This happened repeatedly during the sessions I was videotaping. He focused on clearly and directly supporting the kids through his system of reviewing expectations, due dates and requirements.

Setshwayo also emphasized the importance of creating clear guidelines and expectations with the students. One instance that was videotaped occurred on November 17[1], where he was chastising the kids as a group for being slow in arranging their mandatory community service placements[1]. He very firmly told the group what the expectations of them were, and the potential challenges they could face if they did not arrange a service place soon. He drew this out to them by explaining that they needed a service placement to get their community service credits, and without these credits, they would not graduate. I am providing the video transcript of this instance below:

> See I don't have your contract, you gotta get your contract in... Ok, back to the focus of this issue here,... You NEED to have your community service in place,

this quarter began November 2nd, but I don't have your contract. I NEED YOUR CONTRACT, and for those of you who don't have a community service, you're 4 weeks late. You [*sic*] supposed to take the first marking period to find a community service, and begin it the second marking period, so, if you did not take the time during the first marking period to find one, you better get on the stick and get one. These weeks that you have spent not doing community service, you gotta make up these hours, you gotta spend two and a half hours per week for the marking period, for whatever the length of the marking period, now, I'm gonna give you a deadline.

His tone with the students was forceful, powerful, and also chastising. He reminded them of their responsibilities and the consequences should they fail to meet them. He was clear with them about their responsibilities, and what the consequences were for not meeting his expectations. When Setshwayo and I discussed the "scolding" scene during the stimulated recall in our second interview he was quick to point out the necessity of this with the kids. He argued that if he didn't care, he wouldn't take on the responsibility of reminding them:

> and if… I didn't care about them, and didn't care about the results of their efforts, you know, at the end of the year, it woulda been – "Setshwayo, how come you didn't…." I woulda been "Hey, it's on you, I told you the first couple a weeks…" But as kids, they need constant reminders, as you can see out of a class of 18 people, I had 5 people… half way through the second half of the first marking period, still had not found a community service, and you need community service to graduate. You know, so… I see myself as being persistent, consistent, insistent… on their backs, so that they can get done what they need to get done.

Setshwayo demonstrated his armed love for the students, in that he was not willing to let the kids "slip by". His expectations were clear and uncompromising, direct and insistent.

The directness represented here is a facet of armed love that appears elsewhere in the literature, but predominantly in connection with African American *women* teachers (Ware, 2006; Beauboeuf-Lafontant, 2002; Case, 1997). In the case of my male participants, armed love manifested through these demanding expectations of students, coupled with a deep faith in their abilities and accomplishments. Direct communication is the key to presenting these expectations however. Delpit (1988) speaks to the necessity of operating with curricula mindfully and very directly when working with historically marginalized students. In an earlier work (Delpit, 1986) touched on the tensions between progressive education and the perceived "repressive" nature of direct instruction. She argues that directness has a meaningful place in our communication with marginalized youth.

Delpit (1988) also speaks of the importance of surfacing "codes of power" to enable marginalized youth to learn to operate within multiple territories and skills, which are demanded within the dominant culture. In regards to communication and instruction within classrooms, she stresses the importance of this directness as enabling access to power, academically and socially. This approach also appears in the work of Ladson-Billings (1994) and also through the essays by Black educators collected and edited by Michele Foster (1997). When discussing exemplary Black educators, clarity and directness are frequently clear elements of their teaching. By clearly and uncompromisingly maintaining and stating high expectations for students, in my perspective, youth within Clark's and Setshwayo's classrooms are provided with directness and understanding about themselves and their own powerful capabilities.

Respect

Clark spoke of the importance of respect with the kids in regards to their behavior within the classroom community. For example when students were being disruptive, he stated "Please stop talking", and remained patient with them (sometimes in challenging circumstances). One of the most important rules for Clark's classroom community was respect for one another within this environment, hence language such as "shut up" was not allowed in the classroom, and Clark expected his classes to be safe and comfortable for the kids. During our third interview he said that he saw care and respect demonstrated in the kids by their willingness to help one another out in the classroom. He said that one girl offered to do the dishes every day after class, and help the classroom community out this way. He said they also show a willingness to admit if they make a mistake in the classroom, and then they will apologize for it in public (which shows a level of comfort on the part of the students). When I interviewed Clark, he stated that this was his "number one" classroom behavior expectation, and otherwise, he didn't have a list of rules. It was more about the expectation and the climate of respect that contributed to a successful community. Though this theme emerged solely in the interviews with Clark, there was another facet which emerged only within the discussions with Setshwayo, the importance of race.

Armed Love and the Salience of Race.

The fact that race came up as a topic in interview sessions with Setshwayo, was an interesting and important aspect of the findings. Race did not come into the discussions as much with Clark (who is white). Setshwayo's awareness of race and its importance in his work is another element of armed love. By this I mean that it is a politically informed love, in that it takes kids' realities into account, and acknowledges the power of race as an oppressive force in our society. Intertwined with this is the necessity to educate young Brown and Black people in ways of fighting against oppressive situations. Setshwayo approached teaching as a supportive endeavor, closely connected to his own understandings of race and racism. He talked about his life and the support, nurturing, and care that his earliest teachers provided to him, despite the fact that he was "a blueberry in a bowl of milk" (a Black kid in a white rural area) growing up. He spoke of this as part of the motivation for him to enter the teaching profession:

> so in the X number of years that I had my education, I had 3 people of color as teachers, and so when I thought about teaching, I wanted an urban area, and I wanted, I wanted to be able to influence and inspire, particularly males... I started (*teaching*) late, I was like 30, most people start at 21-22, I was 30 years

old, and I knew my core values that I want to pass on to these kids, that old expression, you know "They can take a lot from you, but they can't take away your education" . You know, no one can ever remove that from you, and so that was sort of my driving motivation… that's been a motivating factor for me, being a role model and giving the message to kids of color, the importance of education.

The importance of "racial uplift" as a form of armed love is evident here, when Setshwayo talks about "influencing and inspiring" other Black (young) men. This is the centuries-old practice of working toward empowerment of Black and Brown youth as part of a larger goal of community support and progress. Setshwayo's discussion (below) echoed these sentiments, with education as a means to working toward liberation for the self and the community, as well as awareness of racism:

> it's an ongoing, issue that you don't need to beat the kids over the head with it, but at the same time, the issue of racism and sexism and homophobia, are things that I think as a teacher, as an educator, as a father, as a man, it's something that um, I must continually address and make my kids understand, how to see it, recognize it, not just in the world, but in themselves.

As evidenced by this discussion, race was a much more salient theme in my research with Setshwayo, and not a strong a theme in my work with Clark. This is most likely related to the differences in their experiences and racial identities, as well as the aspects of white privilege which often prevent white educators from engaging with race. Setshwayo's racialized experiences are part of the powerful motivation that has continued to inspire him in his many years of teaching, and Clark's identity as a white man has not been as powerfully salient to his teaching identity, or his implementation of armed love. Within the next chapter, I will focus on the manifestations of critical pedagogy within these exemplary teachers' classrooms. In addition, the twin themes of hope and despair were crucial elements of my research and my participants' worlds.

NOTES

[1] Community service is a requirement for every student at Parks. Students need to complete 2 ½ hours per week in a community service organization (one that serves a variety of individuals from youth, children, elderly or even animals). They need contracts signed by a supervisor at the organization in order to begin officially earning credit.

READING THE WORLD WITH CRITICALITY, HOPE AND DESPAIR

CRITICAL PEDAGOGY

Critical pedagogy opens up a space where students should be able to come to terms with their own power as critical agents; it provides a sphere where the unconditional freedom to question and assert... Pedagogy also makes a space available for an argument about the responsibility of the present for a democratic future. (Giroux, 2007, p. 1)

I was interested to learn that both of the participants included critical pedagogical approaches in their philosophies, as well as teaching styles and course contents. By critical pedagogical approaches, I mean that both participants were helping their students to develop their awareness of the larger world first, and then the injustices within it.

My participants accomplished this through providing situations that would encourage growth, questioning, activism and working toward social change. For example, Setshwayo pointed to the ways he brings different opportunities to the kids that he says they might not otherwise be exposed to:

I like to think of myself as someone (something) to bring new things in the classroom, I spend a lot of time in bookstores, browsing through stuff, seeing if I can use this, you know, how can I bring this in the classroom... you know, um, things happening in the community, in my Black history class, one of my history professors, Dr.... told me that "Origin of Life on Earth" was performed by a troupe out of New Orleans, and um, I heard about it, and um, I called Dr..... and he said "You are coming, aren't you?" I says "If I have to steal the money, I'm gonna bring the kids", we got free tickets to go, and um, took my Black history class, and it just, they're still talking about it, it was just *phenomenal.*

The performance "Origin of Life on Earth" is a Yoruba creation story. In this case, Setshwayo utilized his connections in the community to offer a deeply meaningful and culturally situated learning experience to his students, in his work to "open up the world" to them in different ways. Critical pedagogy aims to expand our understanding of our world, as well as the underlying power relations that structure it. In this instance, the visit to the performance presented alternate ways of seeing and understanding the world through an African-based lens.

On one of the first visits to Clark's class, there was an interaction between Clark and his students. Clark made spaces in his classroom for developing criticality and agency as mentioned by Giroux (2007). One student brought up Iraq, and very bluntly asked Clark "Why are we in Iraq?" Instead of dominating the conversation, or providing an easy explanation, Clark turned this question back to the group and asked "Good question, why are we in Iraq?"

The discussion that ensued contained kids' thoughts, perceptions and the information that they had gleaned from the media and elsewhere about Iraq. Clark spoke about this during our interviews, more broadly, as the desire to help the kids see things more deeply and understand what and how things operate within the larger world, very much in the critical pedagogical tradition. He said:

> Yeah, the idea is that I want them to understand how the news affects them, and how it's important to be, a daily reader of news, that reading, the media that reading something is very different from watching. It's more active, you're able to discern what some of the biases are.

Clark's class involves a daily reading of the *New York Times* for "significant" national or international events. Clark's focus on giving the kids opportunities to understand their world more critically through reading can be interpreted as a form of critical literacy. Shor (2009) argues (in the tradition of Freire) that we are in a dialectical relationship with our everyday words and worlds. He posits we construct reality through our language and are also constructed by it. He writes, "Critical literacy thus challenges the status quo in an effort to discover alternative paths for self and social development" (p. 282).

In order to challenge the status quo, we need to become aware of it first. The kinds of current events discussed in Clark's class included the examination of the impact of "Zero Tolerance" measures in schools, suicide bombs in Iraq, runaways and the complex issues surrounding the economy, abuse and survival, the influence of the recession, and the legalization of medical marijuana. In addition to the current events that students chose, Clark would give them additional articles to analyze and critique in small groups. Clark pushed students to read the articles critically with awareness of the standpoints of the authors as well as the audience. In fact on the October 26th class, his explicit assignment to them was to read a piece about the Obama administration and discuss whether it was positive or negative in its standpoint, and then how it influenced them and their feelings toward the administration as well. Another example, from the videotaped classroom sessions, surrounded a class discussion of greed and its presence in our society. Here I provide the video transcript to demonstrate this more clearly:

> "But after you do the examples of the greed, I want you to come up with what underlying causes, why do you think people do that, or act that way." Kid says: "Cause they're selfish" CK says: "The act" Kid says: "What do you mean, like the act?" CK says: "Well, if you said, that an example of greed is.... People...eating all the pieces of pizza, that it's a class pizza.... The people or the person who do that, what would the underlying cause...? Kid asks for clarification again, CK says: "Let's say we had a pizza in here and I said...everyone could have 1 piece of pizza, and JJ took 6 pieces" Kid: – "Greedy" CK says: "Ok, but what would be the underlying reason? What are some of the reasons that JJ might have taken them?" Kid offers: "Hungry!" CK says: "Ok" another kid says: "Homeless" (Another kid laughs) CK says: "Ok, he could have been hungry, he could be homeless... he could be... or what could be another reason?" Boy says: "His Mom could starve him" Girl says: "He could be selfish" CK says: "Well, he could also, just feel that he's entitled to the pizza" One girl laughs, another says: "Oh ho oh". CK goes back to directions, "You're

listing examples of greed, an example of greed and why someone would act like that. (Pause) "You'll have one list, one item and multiple reasons why".

These are specific ways that Clark helped to develop critical analysis of social issues within this class. He presented a topic that was relevant (this occurred during the banking scandals in Fall, 2009, where major banks had received money from the government bail-out and then also supplied hefty bonuses to their executives). In addition to detailing this complex topic, he required the youth to engage critically and look deeper into the potential reasons for this problem. He did not offer simple ideas or solutions, rather, he encouraged the youth to consider this issue from multiple standpoints. This helps to foster a critical awareness of the world and the events within it, as issues which are neither simple nor easily categorized. It also encourages the deeper examination of social inequalities which is so crucial for youth to understand and develop.

Setshwayo touched on this in his belief that creating awareness of the world around the students was crucial: "By trying to make my kids aware of their world, you know a lot of our kids are sort of like locked into their neighborhood in the city, and I try to bring them a more global awareness". In addition, the next step he mentioned to foster criticality in his classroom was to nudge his students to understand the power of both the individual and groups of individuals working together to create social change. This connected with a point made by Van Heertum (2006), "Teachers need to do more than awaken students to the surrounding world; they need to simultaneously give them the faith and strength to work to transform the world" (p. 46). In one videotaped class session, Setshwayo was discussing the author Rachel Carson and her book that led to so much controversy and environmental awareness in America around the role of DDT and its damaging effects. The kids took turns reading, and then Setshwayo read as well, from an article about the life of Rachel Carson. In the discussion which followed, Setshwayo drew connections to Carson's challenge to the chemical companies and larger social ideologies, to contemporary issues around global warming. For instance, in discussing the powerful forces that Rachel Carson took on by publicizing the negative effects of DDT, Setshwayo raised questions about public understanding of serious issues. At one point, they stop reading and Setshwayo asked the class who sells chemicals like DDT? There are a few answers, and he says "No", then he said:

> Chemical companies folks! So, if you want folks to be ill-informed about something, you put out this misinformation, that people need this chemical or they'll be eaten alive by mosquitoes... she was going up against corporations, who did not want her to get out there and "frighten people" and engage the public and inform them that there's this hidden danger.

Setshwayo drew kids' attention to the ways an individual can make powerful change, as well as the forces that resist this type of change in our society. In this case it was in reference to DDT, but later in the conversation he drew parallels to the seriousness of the impacts of global warming. He brought up the topic of the world summit on global warming, as it was occurring at this time. Again, similar to Clark's practices of critically reading the *New York Times*, Setshwayo brings elements of the injustices of the world into his classroom. He connected Carson's courage to raise a necessary topic, to the ways that global warming is dealt with in our society. He pointed out that many people don't want to imagine that it is possible that we are destroying our environment, similar to the reactions that Carson received with her work.

Further along in the discussion he pointed to the ways that our own responsibilities for taking care of the world are also interconnected with our collective fate. This example of critical pedagogy connects the past, the present and the worlds of the students through one author and discussion. The theme of the discussion was the impact that one person was able to have as an individual, but also for an entire society. This was a meaningful example of social change initiated by an individual that genuinely changed our world. He said, "I hope I've affected them, you know understanding that individuals can make a difference that organizations (*and individuals*) do bring about social change".

Setshwayo stated that helping to "open up the world" for the kids was part of his role as a teacher and mentor, and his awareness of the challenges they face is an aspect of that. He was constantly pushing the kids to think beyond their neighborhoods and families:

> So, I really would like the kids to understand that it's a great big world out there, and that this is just a very small part of it, and that if they get an opportunity to see, some of that greater world – sometimes in their life – take it. Because it definitely changes your vision, your attitude… and again for urban kids, many of them don't have the same opportunities as a kid who goes to St. Anthony's, or Eastvale, or Johnson.

Setshwayo also mentioned the ways that he "felt bad" for "his"/the urban kids and some of the opportunities they may miss by virtue of their socioeconomic status. He mentioned that he consistently encouraged them to graduate, go to college, and then take advantage of study-abroad programs if at all possible. His goal within this was to present alternatives to the students, and an awareness of a much larger world for them to explore and engage with. Perhaps here in the data we can see both critical pedagogy and armed love. By "opening up the world", Setshwayo is presenting options and stimulating curiosity as well as understanding. He is offering alternative spaces and stories for students who have been told by society and those around them that their options are either limited or non-existent. In connection to armed love, he is also presenting expectations of his kids and telling them of their strengths and the need to embrace opportunities despite challenges around them.

Clark took part in the project of "opening up the world" for the kids as well. For him, this involved critical examination of what was going on in our world. He mentioned the fact that he viewed the school and the classroom as sites for creating change through community:

> it's a family, ummm… if you're doing it correctly, you're creating… it probably is (using the term political) the optimum… environment to create political transformation, within the individual, the community, and what's outside.

During one of our interviews, he mentioned a unit that they did on global warming several years ago, and the ways he worked to incorporate change-making into his curriculum with genuine topics:

I also try to make them conscious that they have the ability to make change, but everything's a trade-off... I had a group of kids a few years ago who had an interest in the environment. So, within the extended class, we looked at... the cause and effect with umm... air pollution and different forms of energy. With the final outcome being, there really is no silver bullet. It's, the only thing you can do is use less of something, but then that's the balancing, where are the tradeoffs, and which ones are you willing to accept for, for which actions.

Setshwayo presented another strong example during a class session. He was firmly telling the kids that they needed to be sure to establish a community service placement as soon as possible. In addition to this, he was explaining to them that their community service positions needed to be with an organization that was giving back to the community actively, and making a difference in the lives of people (or animals). This was a natural connection to the work of the Activism class that the kids learn about activists and change-makers, and also engage in some work on their own to create change in their local environments. Through this approach, kids learn to work within their community frameworks to enact small amounts of social change. Each community service placement allowed kids to work in a volunteer capacity for a minimum of two hours per week at the organization of their choosing. Through these experiences, the classroom and the community become connected, and students are able to see themselves enacting change and contributing to something larger.

This connected to Howard's (2001) study, where one of the African American teachers takes her students to convalescent homes and soup kitchens as an aspect of her class. In this study the teacher explicitly ties this to helping the youth achieve not only an awareness of social problems, but also to becoming socially active citizens. Similarly, Setshwayo planned to take the students on a trip to New Orleans to work on a service-based project during the April break. As suggested by Peterson (2003), "Ultimately a Freirian approach means moving beyond thought and words to action. This is done on the one hand by teachers themselves modeling social responsibility and critical engagement in community and global issues" (p. 367). This was their final project, which culminates in actions based on the year's discussions. Setshwayo expressed his hopes that this particular experience would help the kids:

New Orleans is it. So we're gonna do the Habitat (for Humanity) thing. That will be good for them... We need the airfare and then we could be put up by any number of organizations. Yeah, but that's gonna be our culminating activity.

Both teachers worked to influence the youth's perceptions of the world, to help them become aware and active as citizens by "opening up" the world through reading, discussions, critique, advice, and community service, as well as their personal experience and wisdom. Despite this fact, they would not have termed their work "critical pedagogy", which I will explore further below.

CHAPTER V

Awareness of Critical Pedagogy

When I mentioned "critical pedagogy" in my interviews with the participants, they were not familiar with it as a term, yet they both engaged in it within their classrooms. This was interesting to me, as it is sometimes necessary to rethink the ways we interpret critical pedagogy. It is a particular pedagogical term, in a particular academic setting, yet has implications (and necessity) outside of Academe. As argued by Ayers, Mitchie and Rome (2004):

> There is nothing automatic about who teaches with an eye on social justice, or even what "teaching for change" looks like from one situation to the next... teachers who haven't mastered the Critical Theorist's Thesaurus can still do important work in schools (p. 125).

This statement resonated with my research and experience within Setshwayo and Clark's classrooms. It was exciting to see the ways that creating change, and reading both the world and the word manifested with my participants. Critical pedagogy was alive and well, yet practiced with a different name. Setswhayo stated:

> you know, there was a time in this place where there were drinking fountains one said "white" and one said "colored", and if a white person drank out of a colored, people would think he was crazy, and if a colored person drank out of a white, he'd get beat down. You know, just to open their minds up, to those conditions that existed prior to them coming into the world, and then have them understand, that um, those changes took place, they were mass movements, but there were individuals, it took individual effort to let the world know that this went on, and people would take stands. And so hopefully they can make the transition to see that things are happening in their world today, that there's a possibility that individual and organizations can and will and need to make differences.

This type of statement was rich with the concepts that underlie critical pedagogical approaches and his social awareness and implementation of this criticality was interconnected with his pedagogy. Niesz (2006) argues that not much has been written concerning how critical pedagogies are enacted in everyday situations in schools. In this case, the demonstration of critical pedagogy is seen with both teachers in their classroom practices. Lynn (2006) found that one of his participants discussed these types of objectives as well:

> For him, teaching was about "empowering" students to know those things that have been kept hidden from their view. He used the term *equip* to mean that he was seeking to prepare them for the outside world. (p. 251)

In Clark's class, critical pedagogy was about bringing a larger global awareness to the kids, and helping to create an environment where the knowledge combined with provocative curricula created an atmosphere that facilitated growth and empowerment. One example involved different aspects of critical pedagogy, including a research paper and small group discussions. First, Clark was assigning a research paper on the Iran-Contra affair. The kids needed to look more closely into a journalistic exposé as their assignment. As I mentioned earlier, the discussion of greed and its underlying causes accompanied this assignment. The power of this kind of approach can make a difference in the lives of students and their communities by enabling youth to

222222222

22

2222222222222

222222222222222

view the world more critically. This is connected to Freire's concept of *conscientizaçao*, where awareness of the injustices and imbalances of the world are one of the first steps in acting to change it. As posited by Bartolomé (2003):

> Politically informed teacher use of methods can create conditions that enable subordinated students to move from their usual passive position to one of active critical engagement. I am convinced that creating pedagogical spaces that enable students to move from object to subject position produces more far-reaching positive effects than the implementation of a particular teaching methodology. (p. 412)

In this situation, by encouraging students to read into the world and its events, and to look deeper at the larger world, the teachers were supporting the movement toward subject position for students, rather than passive object status. With my participants, their classrooms worked to create this kind of critical pedagogical questioning, combined with supportive connections with the teachers that are necessary to engage youth in transformative conversations and actions.

HOPE/DESPAIR

> Hopes are realized not merely by wishing them into existence; hope's habits are concrete means that help extend our agency and sustain us as [*sic*] pursue our ends. (Shade, 2006, p. 223)

Hope was something that was multifaceted and complex in both teachers' classrooms, as it also occupied multiple spaces and definitions throughout the literature. There was also the fact that its cousin, despair, emerged too. Hope and despair came about in our discussions through stories and memories in the reflections that participants engaged in during our interviews. Hope was much tougher to see visually represented in the videotaping, but conceptually it did surface. The memories surrounding hope and despair which both participants shared were amazingly detailed. Through powerful stories these themes spoke to the complexities of teaching and interconnections with students.

Hope

Hope was connected to students succeeding, to overcoming tremendously difficult circumstances, and then achieving despite the challenges that worked to keep them in oppressive situations. Duncan-Andrade (2009) addressed the importance of this in a piece that spoke of youth who succeed against the odds as being like roses growing in concrete; they represented beauty and strength in an atmosphere that was not conducive to their growth, in an atmosphere in which growth is incredibly painful because of the toxins that surround them. Setshwayo told a story about a student he knew many years ago, who had been in his extended class:

> I had a student, no one in her family finished high school, and her family had a history of being on public services, and she came here. She was on my Mock Trials team, and I would give her a ride home, she lived in a housing

development, and…I would want to, I'd drop her off, you know, "Let me meet your Mom", she would never let me come into her house. One day I stopped by to see her and one of her younger sisters opened the door, and we walked in, and I could see why. The place was a hovel, it was just… I could not believe the state of this place, the broken furniture and the clothes piled up in the corners, every time she'd come to school she had this wonderful positive attitude, and it was obvious, the look on her face… I left as soon as possible, you know. We were very, very close. She graduated from Parks. She went and got her Bachelor's Degree, went and got her Master's Degree, and she got her Doctorate degree.

At first, I was reluctant to share this kind of story, as it may seem trite, or somehow play into the dominant "rags to riches" narrative. On the other hand, this kind of story provided hope and sustenance to my participants. When a young person is able to struggle, and is able to survive such difficult circumstances, it is a testament to the child as well as to those who have nurtured and supported them. As I mentioned previously, the notion that students could "rise above" their circumstances was a theme that was very important to Setshwayo. In his life experiences, both within his family and his profession, he had seen powerful examples that generated hope. This is exemplified by the story above.

Duncan-Andrade (2009) argues that there are different kinds of hope, those that are false, and those that are conducive to growth and change, which he terms *critical hope*. One of the aspects of *critical hope* is *material hope*, in which teachers recognize themselves as resources. Acting from this space, they engage in quality teaching and interpersonal connections that act beneficially for their urban students. It is a victory when a young person escapes the traps that have been laid for them by virtue of their skin color, location and familial history. It is an act of refusal and resistance; this is where there are instances of hope combined with action. A strong undercurrent for Setshwayo was the possibility that youth have of changing their destinies, and of attaining something better for themselves. This is connected closely to a long-standing tradition of African American intellectual critique of inequities, and the belief that education is critical to the project of "racial uplift" (Jones, 2001; Dixson, 2003; Foster, 1991; Givens-Generett, 2005). As Setshwayo continued his story during our first interview:

> She's (*in*) the school district, got her Doctorate from Upton, and so, looking at Shaya and this incredibly dysfunctional family she came from and when I tell kids, "You don't have to have the same fate as your family, you can change that" you know, that's the social justice, there is that ability to, to make that change for yourself, and for your future. And like I said, systematically, it's much more difficult, it has to be on a personal basis with your students, you know, really light that spark, and allow them to fan it.

This is not a perfect narrative, but it contains the possibilities of change and difference rather than the despair associated so often with urban settings and injustices. Engaging in critical work, it is crucial to notice the hope and the alternatives, and to celebrate those spaces and times where they happen:

> Hope in Freire is not indeterminate but essentially political, as the hope of a revolutionary class and a faith that stands against oppression and exploitation…

Liberation represents history's reconciliation with itself (De Lissovoy, 2008, p. 12).

They *do* reach kids, they *do* change lives and this is what inspires them to continue the struggle, without giving up.

Setshwayo told a hopeful story about a young man who fell asleep in his 8th grade class, many years ago; he was unable to stay awake. When Setshwayo asked him what the issue was, he said he needed to work at his parents' store at night to help them out. Setshwayo talked with him and told him that he was in danger of "just being another pair of hands" his whole life, and that he probably did not want to end up this way. Setshwayo also had a talk with his parents, but to no avail. He was told to "mind his own business". The young man dropped out of school in his sophomore year in high school. Years later, a young man walked up to Setshwayo and tapped him on the shoulder, asking him if he was Mr. Davis. When Setshwayo answered yes, the young man identified himself as that boy who had dropped out, he "just wanted to thank" Setshwayo. The boy returned to school and graduated with a Bachelor's degree from a nearby university. He said he always remembered what Setshwayo had said to him, and that was something that motivated him to return to school, and graduate. This is where hope acts as a beacon, in a dark night of standardization, racism, toxicity, and economic and social injustices. Duncan-Andrade (2009) states that we can see and nurture these roses growing in concrete, and Setshwayo's vocation involves this on a very deep level.

Hope resonated for Clark as well. During our second interview session I asked him directly about the role of hope in his beliefs and in his teaching practice:

> Well, as a teacher, I think, you have to believe… that… well, you have to believe, first, that this is our future, and… it's going to be better. But part of that is also, giving them the skills to transform themselves and the world. They have to… you know, I have to say that every extended class, I feel, I feel that… I'm proud, where I'll, where I'll be tomorrow. By where I'll be… that these are the people who will be creating the, the next State that I'll be living in.

Like Setshwayo, he mentioned the importance of giving kids the awareness and the tools to create transformation both internally and externally. He spoke about hope as being connected to this transformation. His belief that transformation is possible and that it can and will occur in the present and in the future was evident here:

> I believe this place is predicated on, is you're teaching kids… how… first, how to create a community, how to improve themselves, how to interact, to elevate themselves with a group of people, and then how to transform that, that.. the outside of the community, that they have the potential to create… which, if you talk about hope… I mean, that's what it's about, it's that you can change, that you… you can have… (deep breath) I don't like the whole term "You can have whatever you want". That you can have… a full enriched and enriching life.

This hopefulness was something that was delicate and changeable for Clark, as he expressed sadness in the ways the school has changed and taken on different "punitive" approaches to students instead of nurturing ones. This was an ongoing struggle for Clark in his work as a teacher. As posited by Freire (2005), "We are political militants because we are teachers" (p. 103). This militancy resides in a conscious determination to maintain hope and perseverance, even when things seem hopeless. This complexity will be explored further below, where I discuss the more solemn side as well.

Despair

Despair for Clark came in the form of an annual depression in May. He told me that if we were doing these interviews in May, I would see this sadness, and that it was something that he had become accustomed to, but never quite reconciled with. He spoke of the necessity of the summer, as being a time that he used to restore his hope and belief that he really could reach all kids, and enable and empower them to succeed, but that in May, he was faced with the reality that some of them would be "lost". Despair emerged as well when Clark discussed the changes in the school that he perceives as negatively affecting the environment and the kids. He argued that many people in the school point to the students as being "different", but he said that he found them pretty similar to the way they have always been. There is a disturbing facet to the dominant representations of youth, and the ways in which young people are demonized and blamed for all social ills. It is entirely possible that youth and educators have ingested these representations and subscribe to these beliefs in damaging ways. He focused more on punitive disciplinary approaches, and also the sense of loss of community as being factors in negative changes in the school environment:

> I think one of the things we've lost sight of, is we've become punitive rather than about learning. That we've become uhh... focused on a test, versus helping someone become a better citizen, helping someone become a more productive member of society... helping someone become... become a better them... to be able to go to the next stage of development. I mean adolescence is a particular state of development, that if given the right opportunities and guidance, they, they go forward, and we've lost... or we've forgotten all of that, and instead it becomes the standardized test.

Clark's sadness about these changes did not obliterate his hope however. He talked deeply of his affection for the students, as well as his certainty that they are all good, caring individuals with a profound interest in learning. This tenuous balance between hope and despair was complicated and definitively present in his understanding and experience of teaching.

Despair was highlighted in a particularly powerful narrative about student-generated resistance to the installation of metal detectors in their school. I have included this entire excerpt below as an extremely powerful example of the storytelling engaged in during our interviews, and left my personal notes in the text to show my own interactions and reaction to this painful story:

> About 15 years ago, our district put metal detectors in every school. I had a group, my extended class at the time, were very upset about it, because, we had never had violence here, these kids weren't violent, and they were very upset about the metal detectors. So... in decision making, we discussed it, they...

decided they were against this, so, we started reading up on what were some of the things we could do. We read about the legality, read about the 4th amendment, things like that, we read Martin Luther King, we read Gandhi, the kids decided they were going to do a protest. So.. the day they were initiating the metal detectors, I actually had a, found a community service for them to do, so there wouldn't be a confrontation. The superintendent mandated that every kid would have to come.... Walk in the building, get scanned to leave the building. Each of the kids said: "I, I do not have a weapon, I protest the use of the metal detector, it's a violation of my fourth amendment right, my belief in non-violence, (*I had to stop here because I am sobbing, writing, journaling and in despair for this cruelty and inhumanity and disgust that this is still enacted and practiced and normalized, as if it were ok... stopped and got tissues*)

I have never committed... blah, blah, blah.. each kid then refused to be scanned, and they were all long-term suspended, except for 1 kid, who didn't show, because of his future political career. Well, they were out of school suspension, and it would be until there was a hearing, and... it goes on their permanent record.

ED – Wow...

They then demanded that each of the kids sign a statement saying that they were guilty of jeopardizing the health and welfare of the school and the district. The kids all signed it, except for 1 kid, and this 1 kid, decided to continue protesting, and this was in January, he went out every day (Long-term was out of the building), so he was protesting in front of Central Office, from 8:30 in the morning until 4:30, every day, no matter how cold it was. He was there, that was... the superintendent at the time, told the administrators that they weren't allowed to let this kid into the building to warm up, they weren't allowed to engage him, and this kid at one point approached the superintendent, and said, "Don't you find it rather ironic that I am using the practices, the teachings of Martin Luther King, and this is Black history month?" and the superintendent said, "I find it ironic you'd be so stupid as to think there's a connection", and the kid called me, told me this, and my first thought was "I can't believe he said that to him", and I said that to him, and the kid said "Yeah, I can't believe he misused the term 'ironic'"... the kid then went to the long term hearing, at that time we had district values, we had 5 values, and he had put together how each... everything he did, matched each of the values, he did that as a presentation, I was there as an advocate – and the person doing the hearing at the time, finally turned off the... the tape recorder and said "Look, you're absolutely right, but... I've been told that you will be expelled if you don't sign this statement, so just sign it, you're right". Which was really touching that this guy did this... it was also touching that administrators downtown told me that this superintendent told them that they're not even allowed to engage.... The kid was put back in the classroom. It really affected me though, my, my teaching after that, because these kids were long-termed. I have to say that before this happened, I had asked the superintendent to come in and talk to the kids, and present his point of view, he wasn't interested. This was his edict, and he wasn't going to engage. So I learned from that.... Well, and then after this, our budget was cut, and a board member told me that it was directly because of this action. The superintendent had decided... and... it affected my teaching because I realized that actions... actions that were non-violent, and actually the, were powerful learning tools, that, that there are people, and I have to say this was the first superintendent that we had

had, who was punitive, and really, was not interested in teaching or kids. And...
he had... there were many actions that followed that, but it impacted what I
would do with kids, and recognizing that somebody could be so punitive and
have an impact on the whole community.

This poignant and tragic story emerged during our first interview, and
contained aspects of oppression, despair and struggle by youth and their
teacher. Within our society youth are under attack on many levels. They are
blamed and scapegoated as criminals, and they are subjected to laws and
regulations without having the legal rights to respond as adults to situations in
which they are placed. This is especially pertinent in the lives of youth of
color, and poor youth, who are confronted with microaggressions as well as
larger policies which obstruct their growth and development. This is a
powerful example which speaks to these larger social injustices.

It was unfortunate that the episode ended in such harsh and unfair
consequences for the kids, as well as the school itself. It was an instance of
powerful impact and despair for Clark. The indignities that the youth and the
school suffered were unacceptable. This is an important story to tell though,
because of the ways it epitomizes the brutality that can be enacted on our urban
youth, without consequences.

Clark mentioned after telling me this story that it transformed the way he
taught, but not in a positive way, it taught him that those in power within our
district could be cruel and abuse their power in situations such as these. Clark
still carries this story very vividly with him, and there are elements of extreme
sadness, and even guilt surrounding it, as well as a touch of hopelessness and
despair. His story presented an aspect of despair, and yet he continues to teach,
each September he returns to his classroom with a deeply held belief that what
he does is making a difference. Givens Generett and Hicks (2004) touch on the
extreme opposites of hope and despair as being related to each other:

> The delicate balancing act between hope and adversity can be interpreted as a
> sphere of possibility where both the positive and the negative can be held tightly
> in the company of each other. Here the individual can form a perspective from
> which to make sense of life's experience. (p. 196)

The authors go on to explain that the existence of despair does not negate hope
entirely. The hopes that individuals hold can lead to creating actions to work
against despair, and this in turn feeds their sense of hope. Despite the cruelty of
the story, Clark is still a powerful teacher in this district, and that
superintendent is long gone, and the metal detectors are no longer at Parks.
Persistence in the face of despair can be key in these hopeless situations.

Despair for Setshwayo was evident in what he fears for the future of
education, and the ways that he sees youth subjected to complex and unfair
problems in their everyday lives. He spoke sadly of the district in the last 30
years, and stated that things had not improved within this timeframe, but had in
fact worsened through NCLB and inequitable funding. He spoke with
passionate anger about the values of our country and its willingness to embrace
seemingly limitless military budgets, while cutting funding to public education
in the middle of the year:

It's insane, you know, you're forcing this governor to do what he doesn't want to do, 'cause the Federal government, if they just, if they took 10% of what was spent in the defense budget, and put it towards education, you gotta be kidding me, what we spend on defense is ludicrous – it's sinful, it's outrageous, in light of what's happening in public education. So as far as social justice, I won't say I'm pessimistic, but I'm less optimistic.

He also wonders whether teachers coming into the profession will be able to nurture and support the kids enough, due to the complexities of the situations in urban education. In a related vein, one of Howard's (2001) participants stated:

The problems they [the students] bring to class are getting larger. They are not getting better. These kids are dealing with more things in their lives than you and I would ever imagine in a lifetime, and they're getting worse. (p. 186)

In the case of Setshwayo's class, one student in his class had a young child, had broken up with the child's father and was homeless as a result. She missed class because she had to be engaged in working her way through the Department of Social Services' paperwork and bureaucracy. Another young woman was in the position of having the possible diagnosis of cervical cancer, and had been missing class because of multiple doctors' appointments. The sadness of these real life experiences reminds us that many of our youth are subjected to nightmarish situations. We teeter on the brink of hope and despair, sometimes leaning in one direction and sometimes leaning in the other. The most inspirational element that emerged was the fact that despite the difficult circumstances, losses and sadness, these teachers persist in the face of frightening odds. As Setshwayo stated regarding the seemingly opposing elements of his profession:

a lot of stuff that you asked, you never think about. It's a part of what you do, who you are, one of the things these interviews have done, is made me… think, "I've been doin' this for 25 years"… and, and, and thinking back on my middle school time period, and my subbing, and uh, the different stages of being here, um,…. You don't <u>think about</u> that stuff, this is forcing me to think about it, you know, and come to some grips of the hows and whys of it. Why I took this path, and why it's so satisfying, and why it can be so very frustrating.

In the following chapter, I will revisit the specific discoveries on caring, armed love and critical urban pedagogies which emerged through my research. I hope to bring the themes and commonalities into connection with the importance of examining transformative teachers' praxis on a larger level.

CRITICAL CLASSROOM PRAXIS AND CONCLUSION

Bringing these data together creates a narrative of exemplary urban teachers who are not only aware and understanding of their students, but conscious of their role as teachers in mitigating the challenging circumstances that youth face. It is important to understand that this is not just "good teaching", that there are multiple levels to their proficiency and connections with the youth. Ladson-Billings (1995) touched on this in her own work with successful teachers of African American students when looking at the ways that her participants were operating with culturally relevant pedagogy. In her case, she noticed that it was the deeper underlying commitment to youth, their philosophical standpoints, treatment of youth and parents, and commitment to teaching in an urban setting combined with a political understanding of the kids they taught. This was similar to what I found in my own research. It goes beyond "good teaching" in that it is more complex and contains layers of personal experiences, wisdom, understanding, nurturance and a passion for social justice.

Individuals that are considered "good teachers" often contain aspects of these traits, but it is rare to find them all present in one individual (or two in this case). There is also the importance of engaging the youth in critical consciousness development. This connects to the tenets of critical pedagogy, and also to caring and armed love. Through their awareness of the difficulties their students face, they are offering youth possibilities to transform both themselves and their communities. These teachers deeply respect, care for, and support the youth they work with beyond academic performance. This is not solely technical or content knowledge, but holistic understanding of youth. These themes were demonstrated through academics, as well as emotional and social support. In connection to Freire's work, the love required to be effective in teaching involves emancipatory goals. Both the teachers showed this. They are advocates, mentors and care-givers, as well as academic and life coaches, critical pedagogues and guides. These teachers are also technically skilled in opening up spaces for students to thrive, despite the challenges and injustices. This is a long struggle, and the implications of it are crucial to our future:

> We must envision our work with a base on a sense of perspective and history. Our struggle of today does not mean that we will necessarily accomplish changes, but without this fight, today, the future generations may have to struggle a great deal more. (Freire, 2007, p. 10)

CARING/ARMED LOVE

The importance of nurturing relationships and creating change play out in the literature on caring and love. One of the most fascinating aspects of this was the ways that love and caring may be defined differently, but that the participants engaged in very similar types of interactions around high expectations, creation of community, and balancing toughness and playfulness with their students, as well as understanding them. Clark addressed this directly once in conversation, stating that though he knew that they (the participants) were very different individuals, he could also see some underlying similarities in their teaching philosophies and practices.

North (2009) examined four K-12 teachers working to bring social justice into their classrooms, and she found that caring relationships and behaviors differed, but that her participants consistently demonstrated aspects of "critical care" (Antrop-González & De Jesús, 2006, cited in North). These were strikingly similar to the interactions and discussions that I had with my participants. For instance, two of her participants shared food on a regular basis with their students, and demonstrations of genuine caring included taking time to explain, listen, and clarify assignments for kids, as well as going out of their way to support and care for kids outside of school as well as within it. North talks about "relational literacy" to frame her discussion, "Significantly, relational literacy is largely modeled rather than explicitly taught. Students see and feel teachers treating them with respect and, in turn, leave their classrooms with a paradigm of compassionate human relationships" (p. 107). Both Clark and Setshwayo raised the importance of modeling expectations and behaviors in their classrooms, aware of the fact that youth are examining and learning from their actions, as well as their words. Caring is demonstrable to students via their teachers, and reflects the multiple definitions that surround it. As mentioned by North (2009), kids also have a sense and feeling for what it means, and know when it is being shown. Valenzuela's (1999) student participants had a very definitive sense of the difference between genuine care and superficial care. They were acutely aware of how they were cared for and when they were not. In this context, caring and armed love were both demonstrated by the teachers, and understood and experienced by the students. Evidence of this was seen when I witnessed the teachers creating firm and respectful guidelines in their classrooms, acting as authority figures and mentors, and maintaining high expectations of the students.

Duncan's (2002) young Black participants were also deeply aware of the contradictions at their school between the superficial emphasis on caring that was advertised throughout, and the actuality of exclusion that they experienced. Noddings' (1992) work presents caring as dyadic, with the necessity of engagement by both giver *and* receiver. Her argument points out that if it is given but not understood, there will be a break down in the caring relationship. This ties into the conception of love as argued by the work of Freire (2005) as well. In the preface to *Teachers as Cultural Workers*, McLaren states:

> For Freire, love is eminently and irrevocably dialogical. It is not an attachment or emotion isolated from the everyday world, including its tenebrous underside, but it emerges viscerally from an act of daring, courage, of critical reflection. Love is not only the fire that ignites the revolutionary, but also the creative action of the artist, who covers the canvas of thought and action with a palette of sinew and spirit. (p. xxx)

This eloquent quote brings together many of the aspects of caring and armed love that I observed: daring, courage, creativity and spirit as dialogically engaged by both teachers and their students at Parks.

In raising the question of ways of nurturing, caretaking, managing and educating our children and youth as part of a social responsibility to them and our future, I found resonance in some of the elements of womanism. Philips (2006) argues that anyone-- be they women or men, people of color or white, heterosexual or gay—could enact these kinds of behaviors, and connects this to the larger goals that womanism has at its roots "societal healing, reconciliation of the relationship between people and nature, and the achievement and maintenance of commonweal" (p. xxix).

Commonweal, or the good of the community, was something that my participants discussed and demonstrated in their work. Clark was clear that the creation of community based on relationships with the kids (amongst each other and also between teacher and students) was a primary concern in his classroom. His nurturing behaviors included genuine dedication to listening and understanding the kids, and offering them a safer space than perhaps they might encounter in their everyday lives. He also nurtured them physically by providing food for them regularly. For Setshwayo, the classroom community was important, but he drew very direct connections to the ways that youth could be engaged in their local communities outside the classroom as activists, and also partakers of the many different opportunities that abounded in the city. He communicated to them about the larger world, for their own personal and political growth and understanding.

In womanism, Williams (1986) describes a womanist with a variety of powerful imagery, and includes responsibility, commitment, and loving. A womanist is also an individual who is "universalist by temperament" (p. 117). This universalism, or commitment to healing and nurturing the larger community emerged with my participants. So while this framework was not included as an analytical tool for analysis, my findings can inform womanism in providing empirically based examples of ways that it may play out in practice.

Womanism and caring present some very important tensions in my work that I would like to address here. Womanism is based in the experiences of women of color, while caring itself has been framed in white and Black feminist perspectives as well. These standpoints offer incredibly important contributions to my work. At the same time I walk a dangerous line of potential colonization or misrepresentation when I utilize them. This is an unresolved dilemma for me, as my participants were both men, and one was white and one was Black. I would argue that we need multiple standpoints and theories, and we need to develop and learn from the diverse experiences that we possess. If we are to "whitewash" everything (still a consistent problem in many fields) then we would simply confine ourselves to using "our" writing and theories alone, but this is not enough. It is silencing, and does not allow us to learn from the rich traditions and literatures that are out there about caring, nurturing and being socially conscious, which are deeply based in communities of color. The fact that the literatures on caring and womanism are connected to women (white and women of color) is something that is evident in the literature. However, we need to push these conceptions of caring and nurturance, and see how they connect to teachers who are men as well. If we do not push these boundaries, then we fall victim to rigid gender, race, ability, and class definitions that we self-construct, and that will continue to limit our understanding of exemplary teachers and their praxis. This is not to say that we have the right to misuse or misconstrue vitally important research, but we need the ability to push and expand our fields as well. It is an unsolved tension, but within this particular study I see that nurturance and care emerged from my participants very powerfully, and resonated with the rich literature that exists. This literature was based in multiple experiences and perspectives, which contributed greatly to my work and understanding of what caring means and looks like in practice. Understanding our differences of experience is critical, but drawing on them is also very important.

Critical urban pedagogies

Transformative and critical approaches with youth were being enacted in these urban classrooms, despite the concepts of "total failure" that so easily become associated with urban settings. This connotation of failure results in a subtle (or not so subtle) laying of blame on youth who have "failed" and does not take into account the poisonous systems that surround them, systems that can require large amounts of energy to negotiate and triumph over. Ginwright (2006) discusses this as an obsessive focus on the negative aspects that urban youth may display, rather than a deeper look at transformative possibilities for youth in their communities and schools via their own activism. In connection with this, there is the painfully destructive tendency to view urban youth as somehow disposable, and evidence of this emerges on our nightly news channels, with young Black men and women's faces displayed as those arrested, convicted, or accused of crimes.

Children and youth need anchors in the seas of injustice, and teachers can enact that role. According to recent data released by the Education Trust (2009), "Classroom teachers have a far bigger impact on student achievement than any other factor in education, an impact that literally can make or break a student's chances for success" (p. 1). Though the report that this stems from is problematic, as it focuses on achievement via standardized tests, I argue that achievement is just one of the aspects that critical urban pedagogues pay close attention to. If teachers genuinely matter, and what happens in our classrooms matters, then education has the power to be a significant force in the lives of our youth, for better or for worse.

In connection to critical pedagogies, we need to consistently "reinvent" Freire's work, and this study is a step in that direction. The *favelas* of Brazil and our North American cities share many unfortunate similarities, based on the legacies of racism woven into our unequal societies. There are lessons to be learned and important research to be done that connects the similarities and powerful interventions that are occurring. Despite differences in global locations, poverty is violence, and children are being subjected to this violence. Especially in a society that talks greatly of freedom and equality, this is horrendously unjust. Freire's work and critical pedagogies have been powerful contributions, if we can adapt and adjust them to help us view our problems and potential directions toward solving them. Within critical traditions, we understand that there are tremendous economic, racialized, and historical factors that continue to negatively affect the lives of our young Brown and Black kids. Critical pedagogues know that this is a terrible tragedy; we know this is wrong, it echoes deeply in our beings and our collective understanding. The questions we need to focus on do not live in the well of despair, but in the possibilities for moving forward. The empirical explorations of the ways that hope, caring, and armed love operate in critical pedagogies can shift the conversation to focus on the possible rather than focusing solely on barriers and wrongs.

We need to look at what is going "right" with urban schools as a political move to shift the discourse. This is not to say we need to engage in "hero worship" of teachers, but to go deeper into the everyday and find the complexities and the nuances of what teachers engage in to help their students thrive against challenging odds. What creates hope? What nurtures and buffers our youth against the many storms they face? Teachers and their students are in embattled spaces, and to support them, our critiques need to engage in action and research beyond despair.

Other questions have emerged through this work, such as what does it mean to have human rights? Where else do our youth have opportunities like those seen in Clark and Setshwayo's classrooms to connect and grow in their everyday lives? What would it mean if we actually listened to teachers' wisdom and experiences and paid attention to their daily lived experiences, beliefs and practices which involve hope, armed love and a carefully implemented plan of empowering young people to view their worlds critically, and take action? Or perhaps even more radically, what would happen if we paid attention to the insight of veteran teachers (or kids) in the creation of policies? What would it mean to raise our young Brown and Black folk as warriors for justice and equity? Setshwayo talked about helping to nurture dreams and "fanning the flame" we need more flames to light a real fire.

These two teachers have a definite influence, connection and impact on the students they work with. This was demonstrated through the kinds of work in the classroom (such as working on ways to become socially conscious and active) and also through the connections that I saw between the teachers and students. Sometimes there were striking instances, such as the ways that Setshwayo and Clark cooked large Thanksgiving dinners, or sometimes they were less striking, such as being respectful to students in short interactions. These connections along with high expectations were meaningful. The fact that Setshwayo and Clark both had incredibly vivid stories after years of teaching that showed the ways students remembered them, or even the ways that students wanted to thank them years later are evidence of this. This may imply that teachers have a tremendous amount of power in the lives of kids, both their present and their future. This is similar to what Bartolomé (2004) discovered in her work with exemplary educators of predominantly Latino youth. She indicated that, "these findings suggest the power that teachers and other educators, as change-agents, possess and can potentially wield in their work for creating more just and democratic schools" (p. 115). The teachers in my study were extremely conscientious, reflective and aware veteran teachers who were conscious both of their responsibilities as well as their impact. It was incredibly important to see them merging critical pedagogies into their everyday classroom life, and the ways that this was informed by their own experiences and understandings of what it means to be an "educated person", as well as a citizen, both larger-picture goals in the lives of the kids. The participants' teaching was not solely about the technical or even curricular aspects. The dominant discourse of our interactions revolved around the relationships and the skills that were being modeled and learned in class. In addition, their critical pedagogy acted as a bridge to the larger world that could open doors for youth who have been physically, economically and racially confined within our city spaces. Ek (2008) points to the heart of critical pedagogy:

> Critical pedagogy is not a pessimistic or overly deterministic framework. Rather, the goal of critical pedagogy is to empower students, particularly working-class students-of-color. In this way, critical pedagogy is a pedagogy of hope, with liberation as a goal. (p. 3)

The city this study was conducted in is dramatically segregated, and these spaces are obvious even when simply driving around, we need hope here, and we need criticality. These spaces take on meanings, physically and societally. One need only say "City schools" for a host of negative implications to rise up in the eyes of those from outside of the city. There are issues and challenges, and the kids are trapped in the midst of them. However, the participants in my study were critically aware and active in their engagement with these realities, as well as working against them within their classrooms.

Implications

In this era of standardization and facile conceptions of what "highly skilled" teaching means, there are bigger, deeper and broader meanings for working with our youth in successful ways. This includes recognizing the *whole being* of the young people we interact with, not simply their grades, or their test scores, or their attitudes towards school or teachers. It includes genuinely seeing them, respecting them, and connecting with them through spirit, heart and mind together. Holistic approaches that acknowledge and bring in relationship are vital. We see the distress signs in our society, and need to respond at multiple levels, teachers have the ability to contribute to this in powerful ways.

By looking beyond tests and narrow constructs of "highly skilled", we can bring our political awareness, our skills and our resources to create genuine change in the experience of our youth, both in school and outside of it. Freire (2005) shows once again the ways that reciprocity in relationship with our students is of central importance, just as it is for my participants. This connection is the foundation on which learning occurs:

> As educators, we are politicians; we engage in politics when we educate. And if we dream about democracy, let us fight, day and night, for a school in which we

> talk to and with the learners so that, hearing them, we can be heard by them as well (Freire, 2005, p. 121).

Hope is crucial - hope that is not naïve, but active and empowered and empowering.

hooks (1995) touches on the ways that oppositional awareness (as connected to hope) has historically been taught through the Black church, and what happens in absence of this alternative way of thinking and perceiving the world, she states:

> Without alternative belief systems black folks embrace the values of the existing system, which daily reinforce learned helplessness. Mass media continually bombard us with images of African Americans which spread the message that we are hopeless, trapped, unable to change our circumstances in meaningful ways. No wonder then that a generation of black folks who learn much of their knowledge of race and struggles to end racism from movies and television see themselves as victims… Despair and feelings of hopelessness are central to the formation of a psychology of victimization. (pp. 57–58)

Hope requires a determined unwillingness to accept the "fate" of victimization, as passive subjects in a destructive, racist and economically unjust world. This requires teachers to model their experiences and behaviors, and also to mentor youth in multiple ways that go beyond "purely academic" or skills-based approaches. Our interconnections are what keep us going as a species. The classroom should not be seen as an exception, but as a crucial space for this to be recognized and drawn upon as a way of nurturing and educating our youth simultaneously. If we do this, we can genuinely look to the future with hope. As stated by Setshwayo, "And one of the things my Mom used to say all the time, you know, 'There's tomorrow. Hope that things will be different for you tomorrow, next week, next month, next year'".

Taking responsibility as educators seriously entails having hope that what we do has significance, and will contribute to a greater future for us all. This is not naïve, or presented with the intention to obscure the tragedies that do indeed happen, but people continue to struggle. It reaffirmed the feeling that I had entering into the research that teaching is indeed "a human endeavor" based strongly in the interconnections we share with our students. These interconnections are vital.

Another facet that emerged through this research was political. I realized that showcasing these rich practices is incredibly important to do in urban settings, where the deficit discourses and "Urban Legends" continue to portray destructive youth and heartless teachers and administrators, along with decrepit buildings and decaying cities. Many contemporary films contribute to this image, as well as disturbing news stories of "failing" schools and corrupt teachers and officials. This is not to deny that these instances and people exist, but it is a part of the portrait, not the entire illustration. It depends on where we focus our vision, what we choose to see. In this study, hope, love, caring and criticality all surfaced through this work as complex and multifaceted pieces of what it means to be a transformative urban educator. Brilliance, beauty, connection, commitment, and dedication thrive in urban schools, but it is our historic legacy of racism and classism that has fed deficit discourses. In the militaristic control of urban schools as evidenced by extreme levels of policing and surveillance (Monahan, 2009), images grounded in these deficit views are used to justify extreme means of controlling youth and their teachers. Working against this discourse of despair becomes critical, as our discourses shape, define and re-shape our realities, or as stated by Shor (2009), "Through words and other actions, we build ourselves in a world that is building us" (p. 282). In our desire to change our realities, our vision needs to change as well. We need the critiques to assess the problems, but they must not be a stopping point. Critique involves activism through our lives and ourselves:

> Critical teachers and researchers must also embody the change they are advocating, showing students alternatives through their actions together with their words. This requires more than critique, activism and alluding to the Great Refusal; it also must include a positive dream that can inspire others to follow, embracing their creativity and beliefs (Van Heertum, 2006, p. 50).

Despair offers no possibilities, and therefore no potential solutions. Though our educational system may be shocking or even cruel, this is not an excuse for inactivity; instead it is a call to mobilization. We should/can/must hope and continue to work towards a future that will nurture our young people instead of trying to destroy them.

CONCLUSION

In bringing together the various threads of this work, there are intricate interconnections between the themes that emerged. Clark and Setshwayo's classrooms are like bubbles or safe places in difficult times. In connection to critical theoretical standpoints, these teachers encourage deeper analysis of society via their work in the classroom. Setshwayo's focus on activism and Clark's focus on critical literacy practices bring into empirical discussion the everyday praxis of critical pedagogies in an urban setting.

In Freirean terms, teaching the kids to read the word and the world were present here. Armed love and caring were both different in their manifestations, however with some similarities in the mutual respect, compassion and understanding (as well as high academic expectations) that both teachers demonstrated of youth. Hope was like the fuel that allowed both Setshwayo and Clark to continue their vital work, each year, each September, with a new classroom of faces and young lives with incredible complications. Examining the levels of connection and understanding, as well as the practices of both teachers demonstrated the importance of their connections with the kids. They are master teachers, and many preservice teachers could benefit from mentoring from such skilled practitioners (and human beings!).

I wanted to conclude with a poem that I wrote in response to an essay by Bill Ayers, (2004) in which he discusses a question he likes to present to urban administrators: "What is wonderful about urban kids?" This was the response inspired by spending time with the youth at this school:

> You are smart, savvy, observant, direct, funny, witty, poetic, loud, dramatic, quiet, occasionally obnoxious, dancers, critics, cooks, singers, musicians, artists,

actors, activists, intuitive, bright, creative, eloquent, caring, polite, inspired, survivors (you have to be), insightful, critical, powerful, unique, fashionable, amazingly creative in your choice of hairstyles and nail colors, sarcastic, energetic, talkative, curious, resilient and beautiful, (did I mention funny as hell?)

I have some thoughts:

Listen to people who care, not everybody does, but some really, really do. Don't give in or give up, lots of people are expecting you to do so, disappoint them beautifully. Show up and take part. Use your beautiful voices, and your potential. Your life is no one else's. I see this in you, and offer it as testimony to you, you need to see it too. Create a dream or two and nurture it gently every day. Most importantly, you are special, unique and have a role and a mark to make here in this world, that is yours and yours alone. (ED, 12/09)

The poem, like my research, is genuinely centered on youth, despite my focus on teachers within this particular study. Teachers can be key in helping youth to grow emotionally, socially and as citizens. These are qualities that are difficult to measure on standardized tests, but they are much, much, more valuable, leading educators to ask ourselves about our ultimate motives: Are we seeking to cram in knowledge, or to develop genuine, caring, critical and empowered human beings?

REFERENCES

Akom, A. (2008). Ameritocracy and infra-racial racism: Racializing social and cultural reproduction theory in the 21st century. *Race, Ethnicity and Education, 11*(3), 205–230.

Akom, A., Cammarota, J., & Ginwright, S. (2008). *Youthtopias: Toward a New Paradigm of Critical Youth Studies.* Retrieved October 10, 2008, from http://www.youthmediareporter.org/2008/08/youthtopias_towards_a_new_para.html

Antrop-González, R., & De Jesús, A. (2006). Toward a theory of critical care in urban small school reform: Examining structures and pedagogies of caring in two Latino community-based schools. *International Journal of Qualitative Studies in Education, 19*(4), 409–433.

Apple, M. (1990). *Ideology and Curriculum.* New York: Routledge.

Ayers, W. (2004). *Teaching the Personal and the Political: Essays on Hope and Justice.* New York: Teachers College Press.

Ayers, W., Mitchie, G., & Rome, A. (2004). Embers of hope: In search of a meaningful critical pedagogy. *Teacher Education Quarterly, 31*(1), 123–130.

Ayers, W. (2006). Trudge toward freedom: Educational research in the public interest. In G. Ladson-Billings & W. F. Tate (Eds.), Education research in the public interest (pp. 81–97). New York: Teachers College Press.

Bartlett, L. (2005). Dialogue, knowledge, and teacher-student relations: Freirean pedagogy in theory and practice. *Comparative Education Review, 49*(3), 344–364.

Bartolomé, L. (2003). Beyond the methods fetish: Toward a humanizing pedagogy. In A. Darder, M. Baltodano & R. D. Torres (Eds.), *The Critical Pedagogy Reader* (pp. 408–429). New York: RoutledgeFalmer.

Bartolomé, L. (2004). Critical pedagogy and teacher education: Radicalizing prospective teachers. *Teacher Education Quarterly, 31*(1), 97–122.

Beachum, F. D., Dentith, A. M., McCray, C. R., & Boyle, T. (2008). Havens of hope or the killing fields: The paradox of leadership, pedagogy and relationships in an urban middle school. *Urban Education, 43*(2), 189–215.

Beauboeuf-Lafontant, T. (2002). A womanist experience of caring: Understanding the pedagogy of exemplary Black women teachers. *The Urban Review, 34*(1), 71–86.

Beauboeuf-Lafontant, T. (2005). Womanist lessons for reinventing teaching. *Journal of Teacher Education, 56,* 436–445.

Bell, D. (1987). *And We are not Saved: The Elusive Quest for Racial Justice.* US: Basic Books Inc.

Bennett, C. (2002). Enhancing ethnic diversity at a big ten university through project TEAM: A case study in teacher education. *Educational Researcher, 31*(2), 21–29.

Blackburn, M. (2005). Agency in Borderland discourse: Examining language use in a community center with Black queer youth. *Teachers College Record, 107*(1), 89–113.

Bonilla-Silva, E., & Embrick, D. G. (2006). Racism without racists: "Killing me softly" with colorblindness. In C. A. Rossato, R. L. Allen, & M. Pruyn (Eds.), *Reinventing Critical Pedagogy* (pp. 21–34). New York: Rowman and Littlefield Publishers Inc.

Boote, D. N., & Beile, P. (2005). Scholars before researchers: On the centrality of the dissertation literature review in research preparation. *Educational Researcher, 34*(6), 3–15.

Brayboy, B. M. (2005). Transformational resistance and social justice: American Indians in Ivy League universities. *Anthropology and Education Quarterly, 36*(3), 193–210.

Brown, J. W., & Butty, J. M. (1999). Factors that influence African American male teachers' educational and career aspirations: Implications for school district recruitment and retention efforts. *The Journal of Negro Education, 68*(3), 280–292.

Brown, A. (2009). "Brothers gonna work it out": Understanding the pedagogic performance of African American male teachers working with African American male students. *The Urban Review, 41,* 416–435.

Buendía, E., Ares, N., Juarez, B., & Peercy, M. (2004). The geographies of difference: The production of the East side, West side and Central city school. *American Educational Research Journal, 41*(4), 833–863.

REFERENCES

Cammarota, J. (2004). The gendered and racialized pathways of Latina and Latino Youth: Different struggles, different resistances in the urban context. *Anthropology & Education Quarterly, 35*(1), 53–74.

Cammarota, J. (2007). A social justice approach to achievement: Guiding Latina/o students toward educational attainment with a challenging, socially relevant curriculum. *Equity and Excellence in Education, 40*, 87–96.

Cammarota, J., & Romero, A. (2011). Participatory action research for high school students: Transforming policy, practice, and the personal with social justice education. *Educational Policy, 25*(3), 488–506. doi: 10.1177/0895904810361722

Case, K. I. (1997). African American otherrmothering in the urban elementary school. *The Urban Review, 29*(1), 25–39.

Cassidy, W., & Bates, A. (2005). "Drop-Outs" and "Push-Outs"; Finding hope at a school that actualizes the ethic of care. *American Journal of Education, 112*, 66–102.

Chapman, T., & Hobbel, N. (2010). *Social Justice Pedagogy across the Curriculum: The Practice of Freedom.* New York: Routledge.

Charmaz, K. (2006). *Constructing Grounded Theory.* Los Angeles, CA: Sage.

Chávez, V., & Soep, E. (2005). Youth radio and the pedagogy of collegiality. *Harvard Educational Review, 75*(4), 409–434.

Chmelynski, C. (2006). Getting more men and Blacks into teaching. *Education Digest, 71*(5), 40–42.

Choudhury, M., & Share, J. (2012). Critical media literacy: A pedagogy for new literacies and urban youth. *Voices from the Middle, 19*(4), 39–43.

Coleman, M. A. (2006). Must I be womanist? *Journal of Feminist Studies in Religion, 22*(1), 85–134.

Coté, M., Day, R. & de Peuter, G. (2007). Utopian pedagogy: Creating radical alternatives in the Neoliberal age. *Education, Pedagogy and Cultural Studies, 29*(4), 317–336.

Creswell, J. D. (2005). The process of conducting research: Quantitative and qualitative approaches. In *Educational Research: Planning, Conducting, and Evaluating Quantitative and Qualitative Research* (2nd ed., pp. 2–57). Upper Saddle River, NJ: Prentice Hall.

Cross, B. (2007). Urban school achievement gap as a metaphor to conceal U.S. apartheid education. *Theory into Practice, 46*(3), 247–255.

Daniel, B. J. (2005). Researching African Canadian women. In G. J. Sefa Dei & G. S. Johal (Eds.), *Critical Issues in Anti-racist Research Methodologies* (pp. 553–578).

Darder, A. (1991). *Culture and Power in the Classroom.* Westport, CT: Bergin & Garvey.

Darder, A. (2002). *Reinventing Paulo Freire: A Pedagogy of Love.* Boulder, CO: Westview Press.

Darder, A. (2003). Teaching as an act of love: Reflections on Paulo Freire and his contributions to our lives and our work. In A. Darder, M. Baltodano, & R. D. Torres (Eds.), *The Critical Pedagogy Reader* (pp. 497–510). New York: RoutledgeFalmer.

Darder, A., Baltodano, M., & Torres, R. (2003). Critical pedagogy: An introduction. In A. Darder, M. Baltodano, & R. D. Torres (Eds.), *The Critical Pedagogy Reader* (pp. 1–21). New York: RoutledgeFalmer.

De Lissovoy, N. (2008). *Power, Crisis and Education for Liberation.* New York: Palgrave Macmillan.

Delgado Bernal, D. (2002). Critical race theory, Latino critical theory and critical raced-gendered epistemologies: Recognizing students of color as holders and creators of knowledge. *Qualitative Inquiry, 8*, 105–126.

Delgado Bernal, D. (1998). Using a Chicana Feminist epistemology in educational research. *Harvard Educational Review, 68*(4), 555–582.

Delgado, R. & Stefanic, J. (Eds.). (2000). *Critical Race Theory: The Cutting Edge* (2nd ed.). Philadelphia: Temple University Press.

Delgado, R. & Stefancic, J. (Eds.). (2005). *The Derrick Bell Reader.* New York: New York University Press.

Denzin, N., & Lincoln Y. (2005). *The Handbook of Qualitative Research* (3rd ed.). Thousand Oaks, CA: Sage.

Dixson, A. D. (2003). "Let's do this!": Black women teachers politics and pedagogy. *Urban Education, 38*(2), 217–235.

Dixson, A. D., & Rousseau, C. K. (2006). *Critical Race Theory in Education: All God's Children Got a Song.* New York: Routledge, Taylor & Francis Group.

Duncan-Andrade, J., & Morrell, E. (2008). *The Art of Critical Pedagogy: Possibilities for Moving from Theory to Practice in Urban Schools.* New York: Peter Lang.

Duncan-Andrade, J. (2009). Note to educators: Hope required when growing roses in concrete. *Harvard Educational Review, 79*(2), 181–194.

Duncan, G. A. (2002). Beyond love: A critical race ethnography of the schooling of adolescent Black males. *Equity and Excellence in Education, 35*(2), 131–143.

The Education Trust. (2009, November). *Fighting for Quality and Equality too: How State Policy Makers can Ensure the Drive to Improve Teacher Quality doesn't Just Trickle Down to Poor and Minority Children.* Washington, DC: Jerald, C.D., Haycock, K., & Wilkins, A.

Ek, L. (2008). Language and literacy in the Pentecostal church and the public high school: A case study of a Mexican ESL student. *High School Journal, 92*(2), 1–13.

Fine, M. (1994). Working the hyphens: Reinventing self and other in qualitative research. In N. Denzin & Y. Lincoln (Eds.), *The Handbook of Qualitative Research* (2nd ed.) Thousand Oaks, CA: Sage.

Fine, M., Weis, L., Weseen, S., & Wong, L. (2000). For whom? Qualitative research, representations and social responsibilities. In N. Denzin & Y. Lincoln (Eds.), *The Handbook of Qualitative Research* (2nd ed., pp. 107–131). Thousand Oaks, CA: Sage.

Foote, M. (2009). *Test Duress: A Case Study of a High School with a Progressive Mission and Its Response to High-stakes Graduation Tests.* Unpublished Doctoral Dissertation, University of Rochester.

Foster, M. (1991). Constancy, connectedness, and constraints in the lives of African- American teachers. *NWSA, 3*(Spring), 233–261.

Foster, M. (1992). The politics of race: Through the eyes of African American teachers. In K. Weiler & C. Mitchell (Eds.), *What Schools Can Do: Critical Pedagogy and Practice* (pp. 177–202). Albany, New York: State University of New York Press.

Fox, M. (2011/2012, December, January). Literate bodies: Multigenerational participatory action research and embodied methodologies as critical literacy. *Journal of Adolescent and Adult Literacy, 55*(4), 343–345. doi:10.1002/JAAL.00042.

Freire, P. (1970/1993). *Pedagogy of the Oppressed.* New York: Continuum.

Freire, P. (1974/2008). *Education for Critical Consciousness.* New York: Continuum.

Freire, P. (1992/2004). *Pedagogy of Hope: Reliving Pedagogy of the Oppressed.* New York: Continuum.

Freire, P. (2005). *Teachers as Cultural Workers: Letters to Those Who Dare Teach.* Boulder, CO: Westview Press.

Freire, P. (2007). *Daring to Dream: Toward a Pedagogy of the Unfinished.* Boulder, CO: Paradigm Publishers.

Gilligan, C. (1977). In a different voice: Women's conceptions of the self and of morality. *Harvard Educational Review, 47*, 481–517.

Ginwright, S. (2006). *Toward a Politics of Relevance: Race, Resistance and African American Youth Activities.* Youth Activism. Retrieved November 18, 2008, from http://ya.ssrc.org/african/Ginwright

Ginwright, S. (2009). *Black Youth Rising: Activism and Radical Healing in Urban America.* New York: Teachers College Press.

Ginwright, S., Cammarota, J., & Noguera, P. (2005). Youth, social justice and communities: Toward a theory of urban youth policy. *Social Justice, 32*(3), 24–40.

Giroux, H., & Simon, R. (1992). Schooling, popular culture and a pedagogy of possibility. In K. Weiler & C. Mitchell (Eds.), *What Schools Can Do: Critical Pedagogy and Practice* (pp. 217–236). Albany, NY: State University of New York Press.

Giroux, H. (1997). *Pedagogy and the Politics of Hope: Theory, Culture and Schooling.* Boulder, CO: Westview Press.

Giroux, H. (2007). Introduction: Democracy, education and the politics of critical pedagogy. In P. McLaren & J. Kincheloe (Eds.), *Critical Pedagogy: Where are We Now?* (pp. 1–5). New York: Peter Lang.

Givens-Generett, G., & Hicks, M. (2004). Beyond reflective competency: Teaching for audacious hope-in-action. *Journal of Transformative Education, 2*(3), 187–203.

Givens-Generett, G. (2005). Intergenerational discussions as a curriculum strategy: Modeling audacious hope in action. *The Urban Review, 37*(3), 267–277.

Goldstein, L. S., & Lake, V. E. (2000). "Love, love, and more love for children:" Exploring preservice teachers' understandings of caring. *Teaching and Teacher Education, 16*(7), 861–872.

Goldstein, L. S., & Lake, V.E. (2003). The impact of field experience on preservice teachers' understandings of caring. *Teacher Education Quarterly, 30*(3), 115–132.

Greene, M. (2003). In search of a critical pedagogy. In A. Darder, M. Baltodano, & R. D. Torres (Eds.), *The Critical Pedagogy Reader* (pp. 97–112). New York: RoutledgeFalmer.

Guajardo, M., Guajardo, F., & Casaperalta, E. D. C. (2008). Transformative education: Chronicling a pedagogy for social change. *Anthropology & Education Quarterly, 39*(1), 3–22.

Guba, E., & Lincoln Y. (2005). Paradigmatic controversies, contradictions, and emerging confluences. In N. Denzin & Y. Lincoln (Eds.), *The Handbook of Qualitative Research* (3rd ed., pp. 191–215). Thousand Oaks, CA: Sage.

Halpin, D. (2001). The nature of hope and its significance for education. *The British Journal of Educational Studies, 49*(4), 392–410.

Hamerness, K. (2003). Learning to hope or hoping to learn?: The role of vision in the early professional lives of teachers. *The Journal of Teacher Education, 54*(1), 43–56.

Harding, S. (1987). Introduction: Is there a feminist method? In S. Harding (Ed.), *Feminism and Methodology: Social Science Issues* (pp. 1–13). Bloomington, IN: Indiana University Press.

Haskell McBee, R. (2007). What it means to care: How educators conceptualize and actualize caring. *Action in Teacher Education, 29*(3), 33–42.

Hernández-Avila, I. (2002). In the presence of spirit(s): A meditation on the politics of solidarity and transformation. In G. Anzaldúa & A. Keating (Eds.), *This Bridge We Call Home: Radical Visions for Transformation* (pp. 530–538). New York: Routledge.

Hill Collins, P. (1996). What's in a name? Womanism, Black feminism and beyond. *The Black Scholar, 26*(1), 9–17.

Hill, K. D. (2009). Code switching pedagogies and African American student voices: Acceptance and resistance. *Journal of Adolescent & Adult Literacy, 53*(2), 120–131.

Hill, M. L. (2009). Wounded healing: Forming a storytelling community in hip-hop lit. *Teachers College Record, 111*(1), 248–293.

Hodge, E. M., & Ozag, D. (2007). The relationship between North Carolina teachers trust and hope and their organizational commitment. *The Delta Pi Epsilon Journal, 49*(2), 128–139.

hooks, b. (1994). *Teaching to Transgress: Education as the Practice of Freedom.* New York: Routledge.

hooks, b. (1995). *Killing Rage: Ending Racism.* New York: Henry Holt and Company.

hooks, b. (2003). *Teaching Community: A Pedagogy of Hope.* New York: Routledge.

Howard, T. (2001). Powerful pedagogy for African American students: A case of four teachers. *Urban Education, 36*(2), 179–202.

Hudson-Weems, C. (2006/1989). Cultural agenda conflicts in Academia: Critical issues for Africana women's studies. In L. Phillips (Ed.), *The Womanist Reader* (pp. 37–54). New York: Routledge.

Irvine, J. (1988). An analysis of the problem of disappearing Black educators. *Elementary School Journal, 88,* 503–513.

Janesick, V. J. (2007). Reflections on the violence of high-stakes testing and the soothing nature of critical pedagogy. In P. McLaren & J. L. Kincheloe (Eds.), *Critical Pedagogy: Where are We Now?* (pp. 239–248). New York: Peter Lang.

Jones, R. L. (2001). The liberatory education of the talented tenth: Critical consciousness and the continuing Black humanization process. *The Negro Educational Review, 52*(1,2), 3–18.

Kauffman, D., Moore Johnson, S., Kardos, S. M., Liu, E., & Peske, H. G. (2002). "Lost at sea": New teachers' experiences with curriculum and assessment. *Teachers' College Record, 104*(2), 273–300.

Kincheloe, J. L. (2007). Critical pedagogy in the Twenty-First century: Evolution for survival. In P. McLaren & J. L. Kincheloe (Eds.), *Critical Pedagogy: Where are We Now?* (pp. 9–42). New York: Peter Lang.

Kirshner, B. (2008). Guided participation in three youth activism organizations: Facilitation, apprenticeship and joint work. *Journal of the Learning Sciences, 17*(1), 60–101.

Kozol, J. (1991). *Savage Inequalities.* New York: Crown.

Kozol, J. (2005). *The Shame of the Nation: The Restoration of Apartheid Schooling in America.* New York: Random House.

Kumashiro, K. (2000). Teaching and learning through desire, crisis and difference: Perverted reflections on anti-oppressive education. *Radical Teacher, 58,* 6–11.

Kwon, S. A. (2008). Moving from complaints to action: Oppositional consciousness and collective action in a political community. *Anthropology & Education Quarterly, 39*(1), 59–76.

Kyratzis, A., & Green, J. (1997). Jointly constructed narratives in classrooms: Co-construction of friendship and community through language. *Teaching and Teacher Education, 13*(1), 17–37.

Ladson-Billings, G. (1994). *The Dreamkeepers: Successful Teachers of African American Children.* San Francisco: Jossey-Bass Publishers.

Ladson-Billings, G., & Tate, W. (1995). Toward a critical race theory of education. *Teachers College Record, 97*(1), 47–68.

Ladson-Billings, G. (Ed.). (2003). *Critical Race Theory Perspectives on Social Studies: The Profession, Policies and Curriculum.* Connecticut: Information Age Publishers.

Ladson-Billings, G. (2006). From the achievement gap to the education debt: Understanding achievement in US schools. *Educational Researcher, 35*(7), 3–12.

Lagemann, E. C., & Shulman, L. S. (1999). *Issues in Education Research: Problems and Possibilities.* San Francisco: Jossey-Bass Publishers.

LeCompte, M. D., & Preissle, J. (2003). Considerations on selecting a research design. In M. D. LeCompte & J. Preissle (Ed.), *Ethnography and Qualitative Design in Educational Research* (2nd ed., pp. 30–55). NY: Academic Press.

LeCompte, M. D., & Schensul, J. (1999). *Designing and Conducting Ethnographic Research.* Walnut Creek, CA: Altamira.

Lewis, C. (2006). African American male teachers in public schools: An examination of three districts. *Teachers College Record, 108*(2), 224–245.

Lipman, P. (1995). "Bringing out the best in them": The contribution of culturally relevant teachers to educational reform. *Theory into Practice, 34*(3), 202–208.

Lipman, P. (2002). Making the global city, making inequality: The political economy and cultural politics of Chicago school policy. *American Educational Research Journal, 39*(2), 379–419.

Lipsitz, G. (2005). The possessive investment in whiteness. In P. S. Rothenberg (Ed.), *White Privilege: Essential Readings on the Other Side of Racism* (pp. 67–90). New York: Worth Publishers.

Liston, D., Whitcomb, J., & Borko, H. (2006). Too little or too much: Teacher preparation and the first years of teaching. *Journal of Teacher Education, 57*(4), 351–358.

Lopez, A. E. (2011). Culturally relevant pedagogy and critical literacy in diverse English classrooms: A case study of a secondary English teacher's activism and agency. *English Teaching: Practice and Critique, 10*(4), 75–93. Retrieved from http://education.waikato.ac.nz/research/files/etpc/files/2011v10n4art5.pdf

Lorde, A. (2007). Age, race, class and sex: Women redefining difference. In M. L. Andersen & P. Hill Collins (Eds.), *Race, Class and Gender: An Anthology* (pp. 52–59). Belmont, CA: Thomson Wadsworth.

Low, B. E. (2011). *Slam School: Learning through Conflict in the Hip-Hop and Spoken Word Classroom.* Stanford, CA: Stanford University Press.

Lynn, M. (2005). Critical race theory, Afrocentricity, and their relationship to critical pedagogy. In Z. Leonardo (Ed.), *Critical Pedagogy and Race* (pp. 127–139). Malden, MA: Blackwell Publishing.

Lynn, M. (2006). Education for the community: Exploring the culturally relevant practices of Black male teachers. *Teachers College Record, 108*(12), 2497–2522.

Lynn, M., & Adams, M. (2002). Introductory overview to the special issue critical race theory and education: Recent developments in the field. *Equity & Excellence in Education, 35*(2), 87–82.

Lynn, M., & Jennings, M. E. (2009). Power, politics and critical race pedagogy: A critical race analysis of Black male teachers' pedagogy. *Race, Ethnicity and Education, 12*(2), 173–196. doi: 10.1080/13613320902995467.

Lysaker, J., McCormick, K., & Brunette, C. (2004). Hope, happiness and reciprocity: A thematic analysis of preservice teachers' relationships with their reading buddies. *Reading Research and Instruction, 44*(2), 21–45.

Marri, A., & Walker, E. (2007). "Our leaders are us": Youth activism in social movements project. *Urban Review, 40,* 5–20.

Marshall, C., & Rossman, G. B. (2006). *Designing Qualitative Research.* Thousand Oaks, CA: Sage.

Mayes, C. (2001). Deepening our reflectivity. *The Teacher Educator, 36*(4), 248–264.

McGee, A. R. (2011, March). Climbing walls: Attempting critical pedagogy as a 21st-century preservice teacher. *Language Arts, 88*(4), 270–277.

McInerney, P. (2007). From naive optimism to robust hope: Sustaining a commitment to social justice in schools and teacher education in neoliberal times. *Asia Pacific Journal of Teacher Education, 35*(3), 257–272.

McLaren, P. (1999). A pedagogy of possibility: Reflecting upon Paulo Freire's politics of education. *Educational Researcher, 28*(2), 49–56.

McLaren, P. (2003). Critical pedagogy: A look at the major concepts. In A. Darder, M. Baltodano, & R. Torres (Eds.), *The Critical Pedagogy Reader* (pp. 69–96). New York: RoutledgeFalmer.

McLaren, P. (2009). Critical pedagogy: A look at the major concepts. In A. Darder, M. P. Baltodano, & R. Torres (Eds.), *The Critical Pedagogy Reader* (2nd ed., pp. 61–83). New York: Routledge.

Mehan, H. (2008). Engaging the sociological imagination: My journey into design research and public sociology. *Anthropology and Education Quarterly, 39*(1), 77–91.

Moll, L., Amanti, C., Neff, D., & González, N. (1992). Funds of knowledge for teaching: Using a qualitative approach to connect homes and classrooms. *Theory into Practice, 31*(2), 132–141.

Monahan, T. (2009). The surveillance curriculum: Risk management and social control in the Neoliberal school. In A. Darder, M. Baltodano, & R. Torres (Eds.), *The Critical Pedagogy Reader* (2nd ed., pp. 123–134). New York: RoutledgeFalmer.

Mulcahy, C. The tangled web we weave: Critical literacy and critical thinking. In L. Wallowitz (Ed.), *Critical Literacy as Resistance: Teaching for Social Justice across the Secondary Curriculum* (pp. 15–27). New York: Peter Lang.

Ngũgĩ, W. T. (1993). *Moving the Centre: The Struggle for Cultural Freedoms.* Portsmouth, NH: Heinemann.

Niesz, T. (2006). Beneath the surface: Teacher subjectivities and the appropriation of critical pedagogies. *Equity and Excellence in Education, 39,* 335–344.

Nieto, S. (2003). *What Keeps Teachers Going?* New York: Teachers College Press.

Nieto, S. (2005). (Ed.). *Why We Teach.* New York: Teachers College Press.

Noddings, N. (1984). *Caring: A Feminine Approach to Ethics and Moral Education.* Berkeley: University of California Press.

Noddings, N. (1992). *The Challenge to Care in Schools: An Alternative Approach to Education.* New York: Teachers College Press.

Noddings, N. (2002). *Educating Moral People: A Caring Alternative to Character Education.* New York: Teachers College Press.

North, C. (2009). *Teaching for Social Justice? Voices from the Front Lines.* Boulder: Paradigm Publishers.

O'Connor, K. E. (2008). "You choose to care": Teachers, emotions and professional identity. *Teaching and Teacher Education, 24,* 117–126.

Ogunyemi, C. O. (2006/1985). Womanism: The dynamics of the contemporary Black female novel in English. In L. Phillips (Ed.), *The Womanist Reader* (pp. 21–36). New York: Routledge.

Okezie, C. (2003). African American male teachers: Planning for the future. *Black Issues in Higher Education, 20*(6), 74.

Ozomatli. (2004). *Love and Hope. On Street Signs* [Itunes]. Concord.

Palmer, P. (2003). Teaching with heart and soul: Reflections on spirituality in teacher education. *Journal of Teacher Education, 54*(5), 376–385.

Peterson, R. E. (2003). Teaching how to read the world and change it: Critical pedagogy in the intermediate grades. In A. Darder, M. Baltodano, & R. Torres (Eds.), *The Critical Pedagogy Reader* (pp. 365–387). New York: RoutledgeFalmer.

Phillips, L., Reddick-Morgan, K., & Stephens, D. P. (2005). Oppositional consciousness within an oppositional realm: The case of femisim and womanism in Rap and Hip Hop, 1974–2004. *The Journal of African American History, 90*(3), 253–277.

Phillips, L. (2006). (Ed.). *The Womanist Reader.* New York: Routledge.

Renner, A., & Brown, M. (2006). A hopeful curriculum: Community, praxis and courage. *Journal of Curriculum Theorizing, 22*(2), 101–122.

Renner, A. (2009). Teaching community, praxis, and courage: A foundations pedagogy of hope and humanization. *Educational Studies, 45*(1), 59–79.

Rogers, R. (2002). "That's what you're here for, you're suppose to tell us": Teaching and learning critical literacy. *Journal of Adolescent & Adult Literacy, 45*(8), 772–787.

Rolón-Dow, R. (2005). Critical care: A color(full) analysis of care narratives in the schooling experiences of Puerto Rican girls. *American Educational Research Journal, 42*(1), 77–111.

Schademan, A. (2008). *Playing Spades: The Rich Resources of African American Young Men.* Unpublished doctoral dissertation, University of Rochester, Rochester, NY.

Scheurich, J. J., & Young, M. D. (1997). Coloring epistemologies: Are our research epistemologies racially biased? *Educational Researcher, 26*(4), 4–16.

Schultz, B. D. (2007). "Not satisfied with stupid band-aids": A portrait of a justice-oriented, democratic curriculum serving a disadvantaged neighborhood. *Equity & Excellence in Education, 40,* 166–176.

Seidman, I. (1991). *Interviewing as Qualitative Research: A Guide for Researchers in Education and the Social Sciences.* New York: Teachers College Press.

Seidman, I. (2006). *Interviewing as Qualitative Research: A Guide for Researchers in Education and the Social Sciences.* New York: Teachers College Press.

Sensoy, Ö. (2011, May/June). Picturing oppression: Seventh graders photo essays on racism, classism, and sexism. *International Journal of Qualitative Studies in Education, 24*(3), 323–342. doi: 10.1080/09518398.2011.561817.

Shade, P. (2006). Educating hopes. *Studies in Philosophy and Education, 25*(3), 191–225.

Sheared, V. (2006/1994). Giving voice: An inclusive model of instruction- A womanist perspective. In L. Phillips (Ed.), *The Womanist Reader* (pp. 269–279). New York: Routledge.

Shel, T. (2006). On Marcuse and caring in education. *Policy Futures in Education, 4*(1), 52–60.

Shor, I. (2009). What is critical literacy? In A. Darder, M. Baltodano, & R. Torres (Eds.), *The Critical Pedagogy Reader* (2nd ed., pp. 282–304). New York: Routledge.

Sleeter, C., Torres, M. N., & Laughlin, P. (2004). Scaffolding conscientization through inquiry in teacher education. *Teacher Education Quarterly, 31*(1), 81–96.

Solórzano, D., & Delgado Bernal, D. (2001). Examining transformational resistance through a Critical race and Latcrit theory framework: Chicana and Chicano students in an urban context. *Urban Education, 36,* 308–342.

Solórzano, D., Ceja, M., & Yosso, T. (2000). Critical Race Theory, racial microaggressions, and campus racial climate: The experiences of African American college students. *The Journal of Negro Education, 69,* 60–73.

Stake, R. (1995). *The Art of Case Study Research.* Thousand Oaks, CA: Sage.

Stake, R. (2000). Case studies. In N. Denzin & Y. Lincoln, (Eds.), *The Handbook of Qualitative Research* (2nd ed., pp. 435–454). Thousand Oaks, CA: Sage.

Stovall, D. (2006). We can relate: Hip-hop culture, critical pedagogy and the secondary classroom. *Urban Education, 41*(6), 585–600.

Thompson, A. (1998). Not the color purple: Black feminist lessons for educational caring. *Harvard Educational Review, 68*(4), 522–554.

REFERENCES

Thompson, F. T. (2000). Deconstructing ebonics myths: The first step in establishing effective intervention strategies. *Interchange, 31*(4), 419–445.

Tyack, D., & Cuban, L. (1995). *Tinkering Toward Utopia: A Century of Public School Reform.* Cambridge, MA: Harvard University Press.

Valenzuela, A. (1999). *Subtractive Schooling: U.S. Mexican Youth and the Politics of Caring.* Albany, NY: State University of New York Press.

Van Heertum, R. (2006). Marcuse, Bloch and Freire: Reinvigorating a pedagogy of hope. *Policy Futures in Education, 4*(1), 45–51.

Van Sickle, M., & Spector, B. (1996). Caring relationships in science classrooms: A symbolic interaction study. *Journal of Research in Science Teaching, 33*(4), 433–453.

Vaz, K. M. (2006/1995). Womanist archetypal psychology: A model of counseling for Black women and couples based on Yoruba mythology. In L. Phillips, (Ed.), *The Womanist Reader* (pp. 233–246). New York: Routledge.

Wagner, J. (1997). The unavoidable intervention of educational research: A framework for reconsidering researcher-practitioner cooperation. *Educational Researcher, 26*(7), 13–22.

Walker, A. (1979). Coming apart. In L. Phillips (Ed.), *The Womanist Reader* (pp. 3–11). New York: Routledge.

Walker, A. (1983). *In Search of Our Mothers' Gardens.* New York: Harcourt, Brace Jovanovich.

Ware, F. (2006). Warm demander pedagogy: Culturally responsive teaching that supports a culture of achievement for African American students. *Urban Education, 41*(4), 427–456.

Weiner, E. (2007). Critical pedagogy and the crisis of imagination. In P. McLaren, & J. L. Kincheloe (Eds.), *Critical Pedagogy: Where are We Now?* (pp. 57–77). New York: Peter Lang.

Williams, D. S. (1986/2006). Womanist theology: Black women's voices. In L. Phillips (Ed.), *The Womanist Reader* (pp. 117–125). New York: Routledge.

Wink, J. (2005). *Critical Pedagogy: Notes from the Real World.* New York: Pearson.

Yosso, T. (2005/2006). Whose culture has capital? A critical race theory discussion of community cultural wealth. In A. D. Dixson & C. Rousseau (Eds.), *Critical Race Theory in Education: All God's Children Got a Song.* New York: Routledge.

Young, J. P. (2001). Displaying practices of masculinity: Critical literacy and social contexts. *Journal of Adolescent & Adult Literacy, 45*(1), 4–14.

CPSIA information can be obtained at www.ICGtesting.com
Printed in the USA
BVOW02080060213

312540BV00003B/220/P

9 789462 090729